A GREAT
AND GLORIOUS
GAME

A GREAT
AND GLORIOUS
GAME

◆

BASEBALL WRITINGS OF
A. BARTLETT
GIAMATTI

EDITED BY KENNETH S. ROBSON
FOREWORD BY DAVID HALBERSTAM

◆

ALGONQUIN BOOKS OF CHAPEL HILL 1998

Published by

Algonquin Books of Chapel Hill

Post Office Box 2225 Chapel Hill, North

Carolina 27515-2225 a division of Workman Publish-

ing 708 Broadway, New York, New York 10003 ©1998

by Kenneth S. Robson. All rights reserved. Printed in the United

States of America. Published simultaneously in Canada by Thomas

Allen & Son Limited. Library of Congress Cataloging-in-Publication

Data Giamatti, A. Bartlett A great and glorious game: baseball writings

of A. Bartlett Giamatti / collected by Kenneth S. Robson. p. cm. ISBN

1-56512-192-9 1. Baseball—United States. 2. Baseball—Social aspects—

United States. 3. National League of Professional Baseball Clubs. 4.

Giamatti, A. Bartlett. 5. Baseball commissioners—United States—

Biography. I. Robson, Kenneth S. II. Title GV863.A1G52

1998 796.357'0973—dc21 97-32803 CIP Designed by

Louise Fili, Mary Jane Callister / Louise Fili Ltd

10   9   8   7   6   5   4   3   2

THIS BOOK WOULD *not have been possible without the support and encouragement of Mrs. A. Bartlett Giamatti and Marcus Giamatti. Thanks are also due to the Yale University Archives, Katie Feeney, and Roger Angell for directing me to particular publications. Lewis Kurlantzick and Kenneth Burrows provided wise and pleasant counsel. My wife, Bonnie, flashed the right signs at the right time from the third-base coach's box.* —K. S. R.

CONTENTS

FOREWORD

THE LAST TIME I SAW BART GIAMATTI WAS IN THE SPRING OF 1989, SHORTLY BEFORE HIS UNTIMELY DEATH. WE WERE TWO SEEMINGLY GROWN MEN drawn to each other by a shared interest in baseball, even though our primary credentials existed in other areas, he as a classicist and former president of Yale, and I as a political-social reporter, still something of an arriviste as a sports historian. We had numerous mutual friends, all of them in academe, none of them in sports. We had met a year earlier, when I had interviewed him for a book I was working on about the 1949 Yankee–Red Sox pennant race, a book that celebrated, among other things, the radio age in sports. He had grown up in an academic family in Western Massachusetts, rooting (by radio, of course) for the Red Sox, and I had grown up rooting for the Yankees. Rooting for the Red Sox as a boy and as a man, he knew, if nothing else, the uses of adversity.

I had liked him immediately. For any writer, dealing with

Bart Giamatti was a particular pleasure: he loved baseball, he loved history, he loved ideas, and he loved words. At our first meeting he had been particularly valuable in helping me to understand why baseball had proven such an important link, in my case, to the world of my father, who had died when I was young. Baseball was the first thing my father and I had truly shared. That was not surprising, Bart said. Sex, war, politics, and God were adult subjects. But baseball was something that children could understand; it provided the first entrée into the world of adults, and its stars were the first great men whose deeds a child could comprehend and calibrate.

We discovered certain similarities in our youthful passions; we had celebrated the distant universe of baseball because it seemed more comforting and more orderly than the volatile one we were growing up in as awkward and often incompetent adolescents. More, he had chosen as his favorite player the estimable Bobby Doerr, thinking that to choose the Olympian Ted Williams was immodest; I in turn had chosen as my favorite player the equally estimable Tommy Henrich, fearing the impropriety of choosing the Olympian Joe DiMaggio. On the occasion of that first lunch we had taken great delight in the fact that upon encountering our boyhood idols now as grown and accomplished men ourselves—he meeting Doerr, I Henrich—we had liked them immensely and had felt that we had chosen wisely. One of his favorite stories was about meeting Bobby Doerr and his wife for the first time as a newly minted baseball executive, president of the National League, at a Cooperstown reunion in 1986. He had been thrilled to meet his idol and had told him how as a boy, he had collected endless Doerr clippings, turning his room into something of a Doerr museum. The Doerrs were stunned by that, the fact that this accomplished, graceful man knew who they were and seemed to admire them so greatly. "Mr. Giamatti," Mrs. Doerr had said, "you're the former president of Yale—you're a hero to people like us."

Our last lunch had been unusually pleasant. Pleasant because we were both amused by the fact that so many of his former colleagues thought he had entered a lesser world by moving into professional sports, whereas he found it, in contrast to the world of academe, rather refreshing and open. He certainly had no illusions about the power of some of the owners and the fact that, although at that moment they were treating him like the ornament to the game that he was, sooner or later he might end up clashing with them. Then the momentary public relations benefit they were receiving based upon his charm, intelligence, and intellectual panache might work against him. But he liked the people of the game, the player, the managers, and I think—perhaps because it is my prejudice as well—the lifers, those old-timers who had once played the game because they loved it, could think of doing nothing else, and now that they could no longer play, were content instead to talk about it.

A few months later he was dead. Those of us who love sports and want there to be some measure of civility in them are the worse for his death. Those of us who treasured the special quality of his voice—whether defending the broad purpose of the liberal education from its critics or venerating the pleasure of sports—felt when he died, and perhaps even more strongly now, that we were diminished. His was a voice imbued with the pleasure of the game, yet aware as well of the moral consequences of everything that we do in society, that there are no exemptions from our actions. It is no surprise that my favorite of the pieces collected here is something of an homage to Tom Seaver, a player who met Bart's exacting standards. Whether, given the forces at play in today's society that have worked greatly to lessen the game's attractiveness in the years since his death, Bart Giamatti would have been able to hold the line against the power of modern greed and materialism is doubtful. But at the very least, even if he had failed, we would have had his voice, and that is no small thing. These pieces remind us how much he is missed.

DAVID HALBERSTAM

A GREAT
AND GLORIOUS
GAME

INTRODUCTION

A. BARTLETT GIAMATTI WAS AN ACCOMPLISHED MAN. BORN IN BOSTON AND RAISED IN WESTERN MASSACHUSETTS, HE GRADUATED FROM YALE UNIVERSITY in 1960 and, after graduate studies in literature, joined the faculty of that university. A gifted scholar and teacher, Giamatti was equally known as a passionate fan of baseball, in general, and the Boston Red Sox, in particular. In 1978 he became a much beloved and effective president of Yale, where he remained until 1986, when he was appointed president of baseball's National League. On April 1, 1989, he became commissioner of baseball for five short but tumultuous months that terminated in his sudden and unexpected death on September 1, 1989, one week after his agonizing decision to ban Pete Rose from baseball for life. From 1977 to 1989 Giamatti created a small but extraordinarily rich, beautiful, and unique written oeuvre devoted to baseball. As a leader and public figure he was a modest man and made no effort of his own to collect this work, which appeared in a variety of sites and settings, including newspapers, magazines, and personal correspondence. While the search for these pieces has been extensive, not all of Giamatti's baseball writing, during or before these years, is included here. However, those pieces most eloquent in presenting his views of the game and most important in memorializing his work are contained in this book. It is the purpose of this small volume both to make them available to a broader public and to preserve them as unique contributions to baseball, literature, and the American scene.

While the literature of baseball is substantial, the perspectives of A. Bartlett Giamatti were singular. He loved words and language; his writing approaches poetry or, when read aloud, oratory. Like many artists and writers, Giamatti was keenly aware, as noted by Michiko Kakutani in *The New York Times Magazine,* that sports "can provide many of the same emotional satisfactions as art: the reassuring unities of time and place and action, sudden reversals of fortune and a cathartic close, not to mention the consolations of order and lots of vicarious thrills — and all of this in real time. . . . Sports offer a primal drama whose depiction of characters and character requires no metaphors, no allegories, no purple prose; a drama in which perfection is not an abstract concept but a palpable goal — a goal as simple as the perfect hit, the perfect shot, the perfect game."

Giamatti's pieces on the game involve a series of central themes or preoccupations: the relationship of baseball to the history and character of America; a profound understanding of the deep psychological forces on the field; the importance of character, ethics, and moral behavior to the game; and the way in which his personal concerns about good and evil, mortality, and the passage of time fused with the rhythms, rules, and structure of the game. Like many of our forebears, he believed deeply in a green earthly paradise (in America), knew and accepted that it did not exist but treasured its persistence in "the green fields of the mind," where as play it remained eternal. And in the final chapter of his too short life, in the Pete Rose matter, he struggled concretely with the fall of man. Baseball, for Giamatti, was a parable for life.

The essays in this book span only twelve years. In them one finds both a return to certain themes as well as a definite progression, as Giamatti's career shifts from Yale University to professional baseball. And while throughout these years his belief in the ideal and the "highest standard" are evident from 1986 to his death in 1989, the claims of baseball's governance forced increasingly taxing, "real world" moral decisions upon him. The last of these decisions, the permanent banishment of Pete Rose from baseball, was reached just one week before his death. The elegance and probity of his last written utterance, his statement to the press on the Pete Rose matter, made clear that, had he lived, Giamatti would have occupied yet another place of honor, not only as one of baseball's most articulate admirers but as one of the game's eminent commissioners. He cared deeply about the vanishing American values of Honor and Civility as intrinsic to baseball and life. One can hope that his voice, as heard in these pieces, may continue to speak to and for the game.

KENNETH S. ROBSON
Hartford, Connecticut
May 1, 1997

FIRST PUBLISHED IN *the* Yale Alumni Magazine *in 1977, this beautiful elegy to baseball was written by Giamatti in the middle of his life and shows his growing awareness of mortality. He described the origins of this essay to a New York audience present for an evening of baseball readings he shared with Roger Angell and other literati of the game: "This little piece was originally written one afternoon as the class notes for the Class of 1960 [Giamatti's class at Yale]; I was the class secretary [and] I wrote what you are about to hear. It was properly and immediately rejected by the* Yale Alumni Magazine *on the grounds that it was completely irrelevant to the class notes! I accepted the judgment cheerfully and then when, unaccountably, two months later I became president, the* Yale Alumni Magazine *printed it." Over the years many who know of this exquisite piece have requested copies for themselves or their families. Its impact is most evident when it is read aloud.*

THE GREEN
FIELDS
OF THE MIND

◆

*I*T BREAKS YOUR HEART. IT IS DESIGNED TO BREAK YOUR HEART. THE GAME BEGINS IN THE SPRING, WHEN EVERYTHING ELSE BEGINS again, and it blossoms in the summer, filling the afternoons and evenings, and then as soon as the chill rains come, it stops and leaves you to face the fall alone. You count on it, rely on it to buffer the passage of time, to keep the memory of sunshine and high skies alive, and then just when the days are all twilight, when you need it most, it stops. Today, October 2, a Sunday of rain and broken branches and leaf-clogged drains and slick streets, it stopped, and summer was gone.

Somehow, the summer seemed to slip by faster this time.

Maybe it wasn't this summer, but all the summers that, in this my fortieth summer, slipped by so fast. There comes a time when every summer will have something of autumn about it. Whatever the reason, it seemed to me that I was investing more and more in baseball, making the game do more of the work that keeps time fat and slow and lazy. I was counting on the game's deep patterns, three strikes, three outs, three times three innings, and its deepest impulse, to go out and back, to leave and to return home, to set the order of the day and to organize the daylight. I wrote a few things this last summer, this summer that did not last, nothing grand but some things, and yet that work was just camouflage. The real activity was done with the radio—not the all-seeing, all-falsifying television—and was the playing of the game in the only place it will last, the enclosed green field of the mind. There, in that warm, bright place, what the old poet called Mutability does not so quickly come.

But out here, on Sunday, October 2, where it rains all day, Dame Mutability never loses. She was in the crowd at Fenway yesterday, a gray day full of bluster and contradiction, when the Red Sox came up in the last of the ninth trailing Baltimore 8–5, while the Yankees, rain-delayed against Detroit, only needing to win one or have Boston lose one to win it all, sat in New York washing down cold cuts with beer and watching the Boston game. Boston had won two, the Yankees had lost two, and suddenly it seemed as if the whole season might go to the last day, or beyond, except here was Boston losing 8–5, while New York sat in its family room and put its feet up. Lynn, both ankles hurting now as they had in July, hits a single down the right-field line. The crowd stirs. It is on its feet. Hobson, third baseman, former Bear Bryant quarterback, strong, quiet, over 100 RBIs, goes for three breaking balls and is out. The goddess smiles and encourages her agent, a canny journeyman named Nelson Briles.

Now comes a pinch hitter, Bernie Carbo, onetime Rookie of the Year, erratic, quick, a shade too handsome, so laid-back he is always, in his soul, stretched out in the tall grass, one arm under his head, watching the clouds and laughing; now he looks over some low stuff unworthy of him and then, uncoiling, sends one out, straight on a rising line, over the center-field wall, no cheap Fenway shot, but all of it, the physics as elegant as the arc the ball describes.

New England is on its feet, roaring. The summer will not pass. Roaring, they recall the evening, late and cold, in 1975, the sixth game of the World Series, perhaps the greatest baseball game played in the last fifty years, when Carbo, loose and easy, had uncoiled to tie the game that Fisk would win. It is 8–7, one out, and school will never start, rain will never come, sun will warm the back of your neck forever. Now Bailey, picked up from the National League recently, big arms, heavy gut, experienced, new to the league and the club; he fouls off two and then, checking, tentative, a big man off balance, he pops a soft liner to the first baseman. It is suddenly darker and later, and the announcer doing the game coast to coast, a New Yorker who works for a New York television station, sounds relieved. His little world, well-lit, hot-combed, split-second-timed, had no capacity to absorb this much gritty, grainy, contrary reality.

Cox swings a bat, stretches his long arms, bends his back, the rookie from Pawtucket who broke in two weeks earlier with a record six straight hits, the kid drafted ahead of Fred Lynn, rangy, smooth, cool. The count runs two and two, Briles is cagey, nothing too good, and Cox swings, the ball beginning toward the mound and then, in a jaunty, wayward dance, skipping past Briles, fainting to the right, skimming the last of the grass, finding the dirt, moving now like some small, purposeful marine creature negotiating the green deep, easily avoiding the jagged rock of second base, traveling steady and straight now out into the dark, silent recesses of center field.

The aisles are jammed, the place is on its feet, the wrappers, the programs, the Coke cups and peanut shells, the doctrines of an afternoon; the anxieties, the things that have to be done tomorrow, the regrets about yesterday, the accumulation of a summer: all forgotten, while hope, the anchor, bites and takes hold where a moment before it seemed we would be swept out with the tide. Rice is up. Rice whom Aaron had said was the only one he'd seen with the ability to break his records. Rice the best clutch hitter on the club, with the best slugging percentage in the league. Rice, so quick and strong he once checked his swing halfway through and snapped the bat in two. Rice the Hammer of God sent to scourge the Yankees, the sound was overwhelming, fathers pounded their sons on the back, cars pulled off the road, households froze, New England exulted in its blessedness, and roared its thanks for all good things, for Rice and for a summer stretching halfway through October. Briles threw, Rice swung, and it was over. One pitch, a fly to center, and it stopped. Summer died in New England and like rain sliding off a roof, the crowd slipped out of Fenway, quickly, with only a steady murmur of concern for the drive ahead remaining of the roar. Mutability had turned the seasons and translated hope to memory once again. And, once again, she had used baseball, our best invention to stay change, to bring change on. That is why it breaks my heart, that game—not because in New York they could win because Boston lost; in that, there is a rough justice, and a reminder to the Yankees of how slight and fragile are the circumstances that exalt one group of human beings over another. It breaks my heart because it was meant to, because it was meant to foster in me again the illusion that there was something abiding, some pattern and some impulse that could come together to make a reality that would resist the corrosion; and because, after it had fostered again that most hungered-for illusion, the game was meant to stop, and betray precisely what it promised.

Of course, there are those who learn after the first few times. They grow out of sports. And there are others who were born with the wisdom to know that nothing lasts. These are the truly tough among us, the ones who can live without illusion, or without even the hope of illusion. I am not that grown-up or up-to-date. I am a simpler creature, tied to more primitive patterns and cycles. I need to think something lasts forever, and it might as well be that state of being that is a game; it might as well be that, in a green field, in the sun.

GIAMATTI WAS ESPECIALLY *taken with players who exemplified grace, talent, and will coupled with those qualities of character he admired—qualities he himself had exercised when, near the end of his life, he banished Pete Rose from the game. In many of his pieces, this search for the enduring ideal aspects of the ballplayer resonate in counterpoint to what he almost presciently senses as the fleeting and often degraded aspects of time's "corrosion." Tom Seaver exemplified these qualities to him, and this article clearly sprang from his ire at the Mets' decision to trade this gifted pitcher. As in most of his work, Giamatti creates a moral fable out of what many of us consider ordinary events. This article was published in* Harper's Magazine *in 1977 and won a prize as one of the best sports pieces of the year.*

TOM SEAVER'S
FAREWELL

◆

*S*HEA STADIUM IS NOT EDEN, AND THE PIC-
TURE OF TOM AND NANCY SEAVER LEAVING
ITS GRACELESS PRECINCTS IN TEARS DID NOT
immediately remind me of the *Expulsion of Adam and Eve* in
the Brancacci Chapel. And yet, absorbing the feelings gener-
ated by Seaver's departure from New York led me to the kind
of inflated cogitation that links Masaccio and the Mets, if
only because the feelings were so outsized and anguished
and intense. After all, Brad Park had gone to Boston, and
Namath to Los Angeles, and Julius Erving to, if you will,
Philadelphia. Clearly evil had entered the world, and mortality had fixed us with its sting. If Seaver is different, and evidently he is, the reasons must be sought somewhere other

than in the columns of the daily press. In fact, the reasons for Seaver's effect on us have to do with the nature of baseball, a sport that touches on what is most important in American life. Where Park, Namath, and Erving are only superb at playing their sports, Seaver seems to embody his.

George Thomas Seaver almost did not become a Met. In February of 1966, the Atlanta Braves signed the University of Southern California undergraduate to a contract and assigned him to Richmond. At that point, Commissioner William Eckert stated that the signing violated the college rule. The contract was scrapped. USC, however, declared Seaver ineligible. The commissioner announced that any team, except Atlanta, matching the Richmond contract could enter a drawing for rights to negotiate. The Indians, the Phillies, and the Mets submitted to the wheel of fortune, the Mets were favored, and Seaver, signed in early April, went to Jacksonville of the International League. He was twenty-one and would spend one year in the minor leagues.

Seaver pitched .500 ball for Jacksonville, 12–12, with an earned run average of 3.13. He would not have as weak a season again until 1974, when he would go 11–11, with an ERA of 3.20. Yet even at Jacksonville he struck out 188 batters, thus foreshadowing his extraordinary performance with the Mets, with whom, from 1968 to 1976, he would never strike out fewer than 200 batters a season—a major-league record. And from the beginning Seaver pitched as much with his head as with his legs and right arm, a remarkably compact, *concentrated* pitcher, brilliantly blending control and speed, those twin capacities for restraint and release that are the indispensable possessions of the great artist. There is no need to rehearse the achievements of Seaver with the Mets: three Cy Young awards; Rookie of the Year with a last-place ball club in 1967; the leading pitcher in the league at 25–7 (ERA 2.21) in 1969, the same year he took the Mets to their first World Series (and, in the process, reelected John Lindsay as Mayor of New York—a cause for the trade no one has yet explored). In 1970 and 1971, he led the league in strikeouts (283; 289—a league season record for right-handers) and in ERA (2.81; 1.76—which is like having an IQ of 175, though the ERA is easier to document and vastly more useful). On one April day in 1970, Seaver struck out ten Padres, in a row, nineteen in all—an auto-da-fé that has never been bettered. One could go on.

The late sixties and early seventies were celebrated or execrated for many things besides someone being able to throw a baseball consistently at ninety-five miles per hour. These were the days of the Movement, the Counterculture, the Student Revolution; of civil-rights activism, antiwar battles, student "unrest." Yippies yipped, flower children blossomed and withered, America was being greened, by grass and by rock and by people who peddled them. This was a pastoral time, and it would, like all pastorals, turn sere, but for three or four years, while Seaver was gaining control over a block of space approximately three feet high, eighteen inches wide, and sixty feet six inches long, many other of America's "young" were breaking loose. That great wave against structure and restraint—whatever its legitimacy— begun publicly by people like Mario Savio at Berkeley in 1964, was now rolling East, catching up in its powerful eddies and its froth everyone in the country. In 1964 Tom

Seaver, Californian, was moving on from Fresno City College to USC, his move East to come two years later. Here are, I think, the origins of the Seaver mystique in New York, in the young Californian who brought control, in the "youth" who came East bearing—indeed, embodying—tradition.

Most Americans do not distinguish among Californians at all, and if they do, it is certainly not with the passionate self-absorption of the natives. Yet we should, for there are real differences among them, differences far more interesting than those implied by the contrast most favored by Californians themselves, the one between the self-conscious sophisticates of San Francisco and the self-conscious zanies of Los Angeles. There are, for instance, all those Californians, north and south, who are not self-conscious at all. Such is Seaver, who is from Fresno.

Fresno—the name means "ash tree," that is, something tangible, durable; not the name of a difficult saint, with all its implications about egotism and insecurity, nor a mass of heavenly spirits, with its notions of indistinct sprawl, but "ash tree"—Fresno is inland, about the middle of the state, the dominant city in the San Joaquin Valley, that fertile scar that runs parallel to the ocean between the Coastal Ranges and the Sierra Nevada. Fresno is the kingdom sung by Saroyan—flat, green, hot, and fertile; the land of hardworking Armenians, Chicanos, Germans; the cradle of cotton, alfalfa, raisin grapes, melons, peaches, figs, wine. Fresno is not chic, but it is secure. You do not work that hard and reap so many of the earth's goods without knowing who you are and how you got that way. This is the California Seaver came from, and in many ways it accounts for his balance as a man as well as a pitcher, for his sense of self-worth and for his conviction that you work by the rules, and that you are rewarded, therefore, according to the rules of merit.

All this Seaver brought East, along with his fastball and his luminous wife, Nancy. They were perceived as a couple long before this became a journalistic convenience or public-relations necessity. They were Golden West, but not Gilded, nor long-haired, nor "political," nor opinionated. They were attractive, articulate, photogenic. He was Tom Terrific, the nickname a tribute to his all-American quality, a recognition, ironic but affectionate, that only in comic strips and myth did characters like Seaver exist. I have no idea what opinions Seaver held then on race, politics, war, marijuana, and the other ERA, but whatever they were, or are, they are beside the point. The point is the way Seaver was perceived—as clean-cut, larger than life, a fastballer, "straight," all at a time when many young people, getting lots of newspaper coverage, were none of the above. And then there was something else, a quality he exuded.

I encountered this quality the only time I ever met Seaver. One evening in the winter of 1971 I spent several hours with the Seavers and their friends and neighbors the Schaaps (he is the NBC-TV broadcaster) in the apartment of Erich Segal, then at the height of his fame as the author of *Love Story*. The talk was light, easy and bright, and was produced almost entirely by the Schaaps, Nancy Seaver, and Segal. Because I was about the only member of the gathering who was a household name only in my household, I was content to listen, and to watch Tom Seaver. He sat somewhat apart, not, I thought, by design, not, surely, because he was aloof, but because it seemed natural to him. He was watchful, though in no sense wary, and had that attitude I have seen in the finest athletes and actors (similar breeds), of being relaxed but not in repose, the body being completely at ease but, because of thousands of hours of practice, always poised, ready at any instant to gather itself together and move. Candid in his gaze, there was a formality in his manner, a gravity, something autumnal in the man who played hard all summer. He sat as other men who work with their hands sit, the hands clasped chest high or folded in front of him, often in motion, omnipresent hands that, like favored children, are the objects of constant if unconscious attention and repositories of complete confidence.

Seaver had, to be brief, *dignitas,* all the more for never thinking for a moment that he had it at all. A dignity that manifested itself in an air of utter self-possession without any self-regard, it was a quality born of a radical equilibrium. Seaver could never be off balance because he knew what he was doing and why it was valuable. He contrasted completely with the part of the country he was known to come from and with the larger society that he was seen as surrounded by. With consummate effortlessness, his was the talent that summed up baseball tradition; his was the respect for the rules that embodied baseball's craving for law; his was the personality, intensely competitive, basically decent, with the artisan's dignity, that amidst the brave but feckless Mets, in a boom time of leisure soured by divisions and drugs, seemed to recall a cluster of virtues seemingly no longer valued.

And Seaver held up. His character proved as durable and strong as his arm. He was authentic; neither a goody two-shoes nor a flash in the pan, he matured into the best pitcher in baseball. Character and talent on this scale equaled a unique charisma. He was a national symbol, nowhere more honored than in New York, and in New York never more loved than by the guy who seemed in every other respect Seaver's antithesis, the guy who would never give a sucker an even break, who knew how corrupt they all were, who knew it was who you knew that counted, who knew how rotten it all really was — this guy loved Seaver because Seaver was a beautiful pitcher, a working guy who got rewarded; Seaver was someone who went by the rules and made it; Seaver carried the whole lousy team, God love 'em, on his back, and never shot his mouth off, and never gave in, and did it right. The guy loved Seaver because Seaver did not have to be street-wise.

In bars in Queens, in clubs in the Bronx, in living rooms in front of channel 9 in Suffolk and Nassau, out on Staten Island, everywhere, but particularly in the tattered reaches of Shea Stadium, they loved him for many things, but above all because he never thought he had to throw at anybody's head. From the Columbia riots to the brink of fiscal disaster, there was someone in New York who did not throw at anybody. They loved it in him, and in that act sought for it in themselves.

None of this reasoning, if such it is, would appeal to the dominant New York baseball writers, who have used the Seaver trade as a *casus belli;* nor the M. (for, I think, Moralistic) Donald Grant, chairman of the board of the Mets, who would quickly tell us that Seaver wanted too much money, meaning by that something he would never say aloud but would cer tainly formulate within himself—Tom wanted *too much*. Tom wanted, somehow, to cross the line between employee and equal, hired hand and golf partner, "boy" and man. What M. Donald Grant could not abide—after all, could he, Grant, ever become a Payson? Of course not. Everything is ordered. Doesn't anyone understand anything anymore?— Tom Seaver thought was his due. He believed in the rules, in this game governed by law; if you were the best pitcher in baseball, you ought to get the best salary of any pitcher in baseball; and money—yes, money—ought to be spent so baseball's best pitcher would not have to work on baseball's worst-hitting team.

Of course Tom Seaver wanted money, and wanted money spent; he wanted it for itself, but he wanted it because, finally, Tom Seaver felt about the Mets the way the guy from Astoria felt about Seaver—he loved them for what they stood for and he wanted merit rewarded and quality improved. The irony is that Tom Seaver had in abundance precisely the quality that M. Donald Grant thinks he values most—institutional loyalty, the capacity to be faithful to an idea as well as to individuals. Grant ought to have seen that in Seaver; after all, the man worked for the Mets for eleven years. Grant ought to have had the wit to see a more spacious, generous version of what he prizes so highly in himself. Certainly the guy who had watched Seaver all those years knew it, knew Seaver was holding out for something, a principle that made sense in one who played baseball but that grew from somewhere within him untouched by baseball, from a conviction about what a man has earned and what is due him and what is right. The fan understood this and was devastated when his understanding, and Seaver's principle, were not honored. The anguish surrounding Seaver's departure stemmed from the realization that the chairman of the board and certain newspaper columnists thought money was more important than loyalty, and the fury stemmed from the realization that the chairman and certain writers thought everybody else agreed with them, or ought to agree with them.

On June 16, the day after Seaver was exiled to Cincinnati by way of Montreal, a sheet was hung from a railing at Shea bearing the following legend:

I WAS A

BELIEVER

BUT NOW WE'VE

LOST

SEAVER

I construe that text, and particularly its telling rhyme, to mean not that the author has lost faith in Seaver but that the author has lost faith in the Mets' ability to understand a simple, crucial fact: that among all the men who play baseball there is, very occasionally, a man of such qualities of heart and mind and body that he transcends even the great and glorious game, and that such a man is to be cherished, not sold.

THIS CHARMING ESSAY, *published in 1978, captures the internal anguish of a Red Sox fan whose ardor and hope are cut down yet again by the Yankees at the end of the season. By using travel as a metaphor, Giamatti artfully weaves together the themes of his longing for permanence, the passage of time, and the seasons' measure of that passage with the sense of loss, as his team's season ends just as the Jewish New Year begins—even in autumn a beginning. Home, a powerful and complex combination of emotions, perceptions, and place preoccupies and fascinates Giamatti here and throughout his baseball writings.*

RECALL AS THE SERIES ENDS, THE AFTERNOON OF THE FALL

◆

*T*HE OLD POET SAID, "NOTHING IS SURE
THAT GROWS ON EARTHLY GROUND."
HE HAD SEEN THE TIDES OF INSTINCT IN US
all and the flux in matters mortal, and he knew the only constant is corrosive change.

He made of that knowledge a goddess, Dame Mutability, and gave her sway over all things below the moon. He was a melancholy man and sang in a plangent, elegiac tone. He thought he knew it all.

He did not. He had never loved the Red Sox.

While he knew of Eden and its loss, he knew nothing of the fall in Fenway. It is not enough to think, as he did, that only once were we to go east, out into the land of Nod. Such a passage occurs without end. It happens every summer, with a poignancy that knows no bounds, in that angular, intimate, ageless green space in Boston.

There, whenever autumn comes, comes the fall again.

This time I saw it in the airport in Austin, Texas. The day had drawn to a point early and I left for home as soon as I could so as to linger, watching home on television in a place full of people temporarily at rest.

Baseball is about homecoming. It is a journey by theft and strength, guile and speed, out around first to the far island of second, where foes lurk in the reefs and the green sea suddenly grows deeper, then to turn sharply, skimming the shallows, making for a shore that will show a friendly face, a color, a familiar language and, at third, to proceed, no longer by paths indirect but straight, to home.

Baseball is about going home, and how hard it is to get there and how driven is our need. It tells us how good home is. Its wisdom says you can go home again but that you cannot stay. The journey must always start once more, the bat an oar over the shoulder, until there is an end to all journeying. *Nostos;* the going home; the game of nostalgia, so apt an image for our hunger that it hurts.

In "The Eatery" at the Austin airport, the crowd is on the screen, watched by an audience of polite and murmuring strangers, our tension a shared memory rather than an immediate experience. Torrez looks sharp and strong — Munson, never more reminiscent of a displaced football player, is called out checking his swing past the limit. The game of boundaries knows no bounds in its adherence to the law.

Later Torrez would not get a third strike on Jackson, but a third ball. That too is part of the law, the part called equity.

As the fifth and sixth innings go by, the swell of pleasure, of completion, grows. The Red Sox look firm and confident, the Yankees tentative. Torrez has been getting his pitches up a bit but he is throwing the ball, not aiming it.

It is 3:25 in Austin, Texas — 77 degrees and clear, and nothing is wrong.

In the seventh, the Yankees lead off with two singles, from Chambliss and White. There is a picture that says "Hassler" of a man warming up in a hurry. But even that ominous concatenation of images cannot disturb the serene sense that it is late in the game, we are ahead 2–0, I am going to board a plane in a mere five minutes and my heroes and I, after a long spring and summer and a hectic fall, are going home.

When Bucky Dent hit the pitch out over the plate to its nesting place where the screen meets the wall, and three Yankees scored, there was no sound in the Austin airport. No whoops, no sighs of pain. There was, for me, acquiescence, and avoidance, and a sense that an even older law had asserted again its iron hand.

It was 3:30 in the afternoon of the fall of 1978.

I rose and left and went to gate No. 1 and joined the line for Braniff's flight to New York. There was nothing more, no easy answers, and no turning back. We have been sitting for a half hour now in Dallas, where I have these thoughts, neither home nor away. I am waiting for the journey to end, since I heard the final score, so that when spring comes we may start for home again.

I now remember it is Rosh Hashanah, and I recall that renewal has rhythms as old as decline.

AT YALE, GIAMATTI *was no stranger to disputes between labor and management. The baseball strike of 1981, presaging worse times yet to come, occasioned this reproach. It is quite remarkable how in few words he links American history, baseball, and the illusion of paradise and its loss. Later, as president of the National League and commissioner of baseball, he was sometimes chided by his critics for his idealism. It persisted, nonetheless, to his death.*

MEN OF BASEBALL, LEND AN EAR

◆

*C*ALL THIS BASEBALL STRIKE AN EXAMPLE OF DENY-SIDE ECONOMICS, WHICH SAYS YOU WITHHOLD FROM THE CONSUMER WHAT HE most desires so that you may substitute discipline for satisfaction; call it a symptom of the plague of distrust and divisiveness that afflicts our land; call it the triumph of greed over the spirit of the garden.

Call it what you will, the strike is utter foolishness. It is an act of defiance against the American people, and the only summer God made for 1981, and I appeal for it to cease. I do so as a citizen.

O, Sovereign Owners and Princely Players, masters of

amortization, tax shelters, bonuses, and deferred compensation, go back to work. You have been entrusted with the serious work of play, and your season of responsibility has come. Be at it. There is no general sympathy for either of your sides. Nor will there be.

The people of America care about baseball, not about your squalid little squabbles. Reassume your dignity and remember that you are the temporary custodians of an enduring public trust. That public trust began when Mr. Alexander Cartwright took the New York Nine to play the first game of baseball on the Elysian Fields in Hoboken, New Jersey, on June 19, 1846. You are evidently so enthralled by your mucky pelf and your self-serving stratagems that you have forgotten what your trusteeship means. I will tell you.

Baseball began in a bright green field with an ancient name when this country was new and raw and without shape, and it has shaped America by linking every summer from 1846 to this one, through wars and depressions and seasons of rain.

Baseball is one of the few enduring institutions in America that has been continuous and adaptable and in touch with its origins. As a result, baseball is not simply an essential part of this country; it is a living memory of what American Culture at its best wishes to be.

The game is quintessentially American in the way it puts the premium on both the individual and on the team; in the way it encourages enterprise and imagination and yet asserts the supreme power of the law. Baseball is quintessentially American in the way it tells us that much as you travel and far as you go, out to the green frontier, the purpose is to get home, back to where the others are, the pioneer ever striving to come back to the common place. A nation of migrants always, for all their wandering, remembers what every immigrant never forgets: that you may leave home but if you forget where home is, you are truly lost and without hope.

It is, this grand game, no game but a work of art fashioned to remind us that we all began in the great green Elysian Field of the New World, with all its terrors and promises.

Today, in those enclosed green spaces in the middle of cities, under smoky skies, after days that weigh heavy either because of work or because of no work, the game reminds the people who gather at that field in the city of the best hopes and freest moments we can have. The obligation to continue to be the medium for hope, in the season America now is in, is an obligation far weightier than your mercantile spats.

Princelings and Sovereignlets of baseball, you speak of the game as an industry. That is your right. Play the game for whatever mercenary motives you wish. But remember that, from our point of view, you play it so that we may all remember a past—graceful, energetic, free in the order and law of a green field—that never was.

Whatever your ordinary motives, remember that you are entrusted by America with baseball so that we, during the deep, resonant pauses, may play the game in our heads—the only place it truly endures—and that we play it and keep it there for one transcendent reason: that we may think well of ourselves and of our neighbors. You play baseball so that we may remember the future we want for our children, the future that always begins for Americans in the summer of the Elysian Field.

Men of baseball, you try our patience. Enough is now enough. Go back to work. You will lose a country if you impose autumn on a people who need and deserve a summer without yet another denial.

THIS MOVING AND *scholarly essay resulted from an invitation Giamatti received to address the Massachusetts Historical Society in 1985. With effortless, poetic prose he weaves together the joint and separate histories of America and its national pastime. His emphasis on the "fit" between baseball and the qualities of the American character are profound and provocative. Unique to Giamatti's perspective on baseball is his appreciation of the unspoken, and probably unconscious, psychological appeal of the game's timeless, cyclical rhythms and its symbolic and literal journey "home" to a people constantly on the move.*

BASEBALL AND THE AMERICAN CHARACTER

---◆---

I THANK THE MASSACHUSETTS HISTORICAL *SOCIETY, ITS SPEAKERS COMMITTEE, AND, PARTICULARLY, ITS GRACIOUS AND LEARNED* director, Mr. Tucker, for the invitation to speak to you tonight. I sense keenly my unworthiness to address the topic set me—"Baseball and the American Character"—because while an enthusiast about both, I am no expert on baseball, or the American character. I could not, however, resist Mr. Tucker's invitation, which opened by asking "Can we lure you back to your native city this fall. . . ." For what is baseball, and indeed so much of the American experience, about but looking for home? *Nostos,* the desire to return home, gives us a nation of immigrants always migrating in search of home; gives us the American desire to start over in the great green garden, Eden or Canaan, of the New World; gives us the concept of a settled home base and thus, the distance to frontiers; gives us a belief in individual assertion that finds its fulfillment in aggregation, a grouping with the like-minded and similarly driven; gives us our sentimental awe of old ways. The hunger for home makes the green geometry of the baseball field more than simply a metaphor for the American experience and character; the baseball field and the game that sanctifies boundaries, rules, and law and engages cunning, theft, and guile; that exalts energy, opportunism, and execution while paying lip service to management, strategy, and long-range planning, is closer to an embodiment of American life than to the mere sporting image of it.

◆ ◆ ◆

In all its complementary contradictions, its play of antitheses, baseball captured a continent bounded to east and west by oceans, laced by mountains and rivers, dry, fertile, wet, wooded, and at its heart, or stomach, endlessly flat. America is a topography mythologized by its inhabitants as they crossed and re-crossed it into an image of themselves, diverse, demanding, unified by common acts of consent to a government of themselves, a government consciously checked and balanced, the formal antitheses of the state reflecting and shaping the inclusive ideals and isolationist tendencies of a people receptive and wary. It is a land simultaneously perceived as a field and a park, as a wilderness and a paradise, as raw material endlessly available and an enclosure infinitely significant. The inhabitants of such a land produce high principle easily and endlessly, as a form of native handicraft. We are capable of investing any principle with the systematic coherence, spiritual luminosity, and transcendent character of a religious belief as long as it seems to promise coherence, as long as it may bind us up so that we may go our separate ways.

In *Democracy in America,* de Tocqueville characterizes this capacity when he shrewdly says, "The Americans have combated [*sic*] by free institutions the tendency of equality to keep men asunder and they have subdued it" (I. 589). Here we are led to America's moral hunger for egalitarian collectivity, which impels us as individuals to aggregate and to invest the aggregation with numinous meaning, over and over again, as if for the first time every time. This American capacity for religious awe, especially applied to our social and political life, at first enchants and then appalls those from other cultures. They find it difficult to comprehend how so many different institutions can be laden with significance akin to religious value merely in order to expunge class and other distinctions and to promote and protect egalitarian diversity.

If such may be at least suggested by a quick look at a sympathetic French observer in the 1830s and 1840s, what can we learn of ourselves from an observer who did not visit and leave, but who left and visited? In 1877, Henry James published *The American*. The hero is Christopher Newman, and we meet him in the Louvre. The year is 1868. The confrontation between the new American man and the old world, urban and aesthetic in its values, is initially less striking than the contraries embodied in Newman himself. "His eye," says James, "was full of contradictory suggestions: and though it was by no means the glowing orb of romance, you could find in it almost anything you looked for. Frigid yet friendly, frank yet cautious, shrewd yet credulous, positive yet skeptical, confident yet shy, extremely intelligent and extremely good-humoured, there was something vaguely defiant in its concessions and something profoundly reassuring in its reserves" (Boston, 1907, p. 4).

James sees all the contradictions in his American, from frank oppositions yoked by "yet," to subtle blends of "defiant . . . concessions" and "reassuring . . . reserves." In this eye, this *Ego americanus,* there are contraries more complex and tensions more clear than in the generalizing characterizations of de Tocqueville. But the French visitor wrote in the glow of promise, in the 1830s and 1840s, when institutional coherence seemed to subdue the centripetal force of equality. James writes in the 1870s. By then the promise of a more perfect Union had been broken by a savage Civil War. Now America would, once again, be compelled to compose or re-compose herself in the aftermath of division and upheaval; once again, free institutions would have to play the role of subduing the tendency equals have to be asunder.

Now there was no escaping the gap between America's promises and her execution of them. Post–Civil War America was complex in darker and subtler ways than de Tocqueville could have foreseen. The matter of race would now forever claim the American conscience, if not its consciousness, and that compound whose mix forms the American character— of moral energy and pragmatic efficiency, optimism and guile, respect for law, admiration for the maverick, and love of the underdog—would be forever changed.

But where in all this is baseball? It is amidst it all. Baseball spans the nineteenth century, its origins and first examples antebellum, its growth and first golden age coterminous with Reconstruction and the period through the First World War. Baseball grew in the surge to fraternalism, to fraternal societies, sodalities, associations, and aggregations that followed the fratricide. Baseball showed who had won the war and where the country was building, which was in the industrial cities of the North. It was a conservative game, remembering its origins or even making up origins (as in the myth of Abner Doubleday and the invention of the game in 1839 in

Cooperstown, a legend created at a banquet at Delmonico's in New York City in 1889). In a fashion typically American, baseball carried a lore at variance with its behavior; it promoted its self-image as green game while it became a business. That gap in baseball between first promise and eventual execution is with us to this day, as it is with us in so many other ways.

Baseball was Janus, looking both ways by the 1860s. One face looked back at all the varied and original images of the country as a wilderness becoming a garden. This imagery, superbly elucidated by George Huntston Williams in *Paradise and Wilderness in Christian Thought,* runs through New England Puritanism, German Pietism, Quakerism, Mormonism, Black American spirituals, and the great debates on wilderness vs. conservation; it has been addressed in various contexts by such scholars as Henry Nash Smith, Leo Marx, and Roderick Nash, to mention a few. One cannot underestimate the power, whether derived from biblical images or classical, of the image of the enclosed green space (reified as well in such variety, from the same sources and with the same impact, on our campuses) on the American mind. Such imagery may be one reason why now almost forty-five million people a summer flow to baseball parks in the midst of urban wildernesses, flow in big cities to a place where perfection does not exist but which recalls in some distant way the place that promised perfection and whose name we derive from the enclosed park of the Persian king, paradise.

Do other American games, also played on green fields, have the same hold? In part, they do; in part, they cannot because they do not reach back to our origins the way baseball does. On April 17, 1778, George Ewing, a soldier in the Continental Army at Valley Forge, records in his diary that he played in a game of "base." In 1786, a Princeton student describes a game of "baste ball" on the campus. How could it be? Because in 1744 John Newberry published in London *A Little Pretty Pocket-Book* that contained a rhymed description of "base-ball" and a woodcut showing three boys standing at posts arranged in a diamond shape. Newberry's book was reprinted in America up to 1787. Americans played other ball games, Dutch "stool-ball," old cat, old-one cat, towne-ball, round-ball, and, derived from English rounders, what were called the "New York" and "Massachusetts" games. "By the early nineteenth century," says Harold Seymour in his excellent history of baseball, to which I am throughout indebted, "these simple, informal ball games were a common sight on village greens and college campuses, especially in the more settled areas of New York and New England, for it was only when communities became established and enjoyed a certain amount of leisure that ball games could flourish."

In 1834, Robin Carver published for children *The Book of Sports* (Boston) and called the game "Base, or Goal Ball"; in 1835, *The Boys and Girls Book of Sports* (Providence) established that a "feeder" tossed a ball underhand to a "striker"; if the striker missed three times with his hoe handle or stick, he was out; if he hit the ball behind him, he was out, if he hit the ball and it was caught, he was out; if he was hit by a thrown ball while running the bases, he was out. The striker ran the bases clockwise. In 1839, the rule became fixed that one runs counterclockwise. Time does not matter in baseball.

Thus, people were playing something called base-ball before the birth of the Republic. Within ten years of Jefferson's death, the early outlines of the game and some of its fearful symmetry (3 bases, 3 strikes) were in existence. Within fifty more years, the modern game in its essentials was set. But back there, before the Civil War, the new country experimented with the game.

On June 19, 1846, Alexander Cartwright led the Knickerbocker Base Ball Club of New York to play the New York Nine. We should regard this as the first modern baseball game. The Knickerbockers were a social club of young men in various professions and trades who were as interested in dining well as in playing well and who had even more elaborate rules for socializing than for baseball. They did, however, play according to a set of rules they had established, and thus the New York game became modern baseball. As Seymour sums up the Knickerbocker's contribution, they established: "The four-base diamond; ninety-foot basepaths; three out, all out; batting in rotation; throwing out runners or touching them; nine-man teams, with each player covering a defined position; the location of the pitcher's box in relation to the diamond as a whole," and they established the absolute authority of the umpire (I, 18; 19–20). On June 19, 1846, the Knickerbockers lost 23–1; the contest lasted only four innings. But the game was permanently shaped. And, given my view of the congruence between America's deepest dreams and baseball, I never cease to marvel that by some splendid serendipity (or is it Providence?) the lovely, open tract fronting the Hudson and surrounded by woods, in Hoboken, where the Knickerbockers played on that June day, and always played, was called Elysian Field. The Biblical imagery of wilderness and garden from Genesis, the Canticles, Revelation 12 is caught up in the image of Elysium. It is meet and right that this place is the birthplace of our game.

After the Civil War, baseball exploded. Between 1876 and 1902, there were five, perhaps six, major league circuits—the National League (including from '92–'99 the consolidated 12-Club League), the American Association (1882–1892), Union Association (1884), Player's League (1890), and the

American League. There was, therefore, at least one major league club in Altoona, Baltimore, Boston, Brooklyn, Buffalo, Chicago, Cincinnati, Cleveland, Columbus, Detroit, Hartford, Indianapolis, Kansas City, Louisville, Milwaukee, New York, Philadelphia, Pittsburgh, Providence, Richmond, Rochester, St. Louis, St. Paul, Syracuse, Troy, Washington, Wilmington, and Worcester. With few exceptions, to the victors of the war belonged the game.

Baseball became professional, gaudy, rowdy, and exciting. Skills developed, playing fields appeared everywhere, it swept the country and invaded the Caribbean and Central America. Cartwright took the game to Hawaii. The clergy approved, the president and Congress discovered they were fans, and the average person could not get enough. *Harper's Magazine,* 1886: ". . . the fascination of the game has seized upon the American people, irrespective of age, sex, or other condition." *Sporting News,* 1891: "No game has taken so strong a hold on Americans as baseball." Why? What accounts for this love affair between America and baseball that has matured and changed but never died?

Mark Twain hints at something when he says of baseball that it had become "the very symbol, the outward and visible expression of the drive and push and rush and struggle of the raging, tearing, booming nineteenth century" (Seymour, I. 345). Baseball became business as Business and wealth and population boomed across the country, as millions of immigrants poured in, as the tempo of life quickened and the country flexed its muscles. Baseball, increasingly played with increasing skill, caught the mood of America and rode it. But still one asks—why?

I think the answer lies in the convergence of many points we have touched upon. For those native to America, particularly in cities, the game, whether watched or played, recalled the earlier, rural America, a more youthful, less bitterly knowing country; for the immigrant, the game was a club to belong to, another fraternal organization, a common language in a strange land. For so much of expanding and expansive America, the game was a free institution with something for everyone.

To the working man, it was cheap to watch, cheap to play.

One did not need to own property or a horse or a shell to participate. The players themselves tended to come from working America, and the game became rough, profane, strenuous, more exciting, and so did the crowds. But baseball had genteel origins, at least in its pre–Civil War version; the young gentlemen of the Knickerbocker Base Ball Club, the New York Nine, and their host of imitators did not often play professional ball, but they played in schools and colleges, with clubs and associations; and the educated or well-to-do never lost their taste for baseball.

Baseball was not dangerous, like prizefighting or football. As we know from the early game books, girls and boys could play; indeed, anyone could, for you did not have to be extra big or extra strong or extra fast. Nor was it especially difficult. No arcane skill was required. In fact, to watch or play the only requirement was desire, desire to participate, to be part of the throng, the singing, the shouting, the swearing, the camaraderie, the noise, the sunshine. It was neither chic nor déclassé to care about baseball. It was simply part of being an American, for no one else had a game anything like it, any more than they had a country as raw, promising, and strong as America.

If you did not watch or play baseball, you could read about it. Newspapers grew with the sport, sports papers came into existence; sports writing flowered as baseball enriched the language and the language developed a vast subcontinent of circumlocutions, euphemisms, and new coinages for baseball. Vivid, opinionated, salty, redolent journalism matched the game. The reader found the box score; the box score provided the diamond in the mind, and, more importantly, gave statistics, data, arithmetic permutation, lore masquerading as quantifiable reality, history that the mind could encompass and retain. Baseball as scripture was born and developed. Then, as now, intellectuals could moralize about baseball; writers and poets could rhapsodize and mythologize; journalists could cover a story with a beginning, middle, and end, and a world of colorful characters, nicknames only matched by mobsters, and communal significance. No one who wanted to be in was left out. As America opened her arms to the foreign born and healed the wounds of the war, baseball embraced all classes, conditions, regions.

Never was a game better matched to its season, or better, never was a season—from spring to early autumn—better matched by a game. The game was outdoors, on grass, in the sun. It began at winter's end, and ended before frost. It made the most of high skies, clement weather, and the times of planting and growth. Until the advent of lights, then domed stadia and artificial turf, baseball was earthbound in the sense of using the earth and climate to advantage and the rhythms of light, shadow, and dusk and spring, summer, and early fall as part of itself. To be earthbound in such a fashion is, to me, pure heaven.

Baseball did not defy the elements. Excessive rain was respected; high wind was lamented; snow eschewed. Unlike football, whose industrial origins and organization force it to pretend to ignore nature, and unlike basketball, the urban game fitted best for small, indoor spaces, baseball in its true state respects natural occurrences and has adapted itself to nature's deep cycles of renewal. Baseball is at home in the natural world, mindful of its own fragility, respectful of the elements, almost civilized in its regard for the safety of its players, careful as it can be of the comfort of spectators.

Genteel in its American origins, proletarian in its development, egalitarian in its demands and appeal, effortless in its adaptation to nature, raucous, hard-nosed, and glamorous as a profession, expanding with the country like fingers unfolding from a fist, image of a lost past, evergreen reminder of America's best promises, baseball fits America. Above all, it fits so well because it embodies the antithetical, complementary interplay of individual and group that we so love, and because it conserves our longing for the rule of law while licensing our resentment of law givers.

Baseball, the opportunist's game, puts a tremendous premium on the individual, who must be able to react instantly on offense and defense and who must be able to hit, run, throw, field. Specialization obviously exists, but, in general, baseball players are meant to be skilled generalists. The "designated hitter" is so offensive because it violates this basic characteristic of the game. Players are also sufficiently physically separated on the field so that the individual cannot hide from clear responsibility in a crowd, as in football or Congress. The object, the ball, and what the individual must do are obvious to all, and each player's skill, initiative, zest, and poise are highlighted.

Individual merit and self-reliance are the bedrock of baseball, never more so than in the fundamental acts of delivering, and attempting to hit, the ball. Every game recommences every time a pitcher pitches and a batter swings. But before a swing or not-swing can trigger the vast grid of mental and physical adjustments that must proceed with every pitch, there is the basic confrontation between two lone individuals. It is primitive in its starkness. A man on a hill prepares to throw a rock at a man slightly below him, not far away, who holds a club. First, fear must be overcome; no one finally knows where the pitched ball, or hit ball, will go. Most of the time control, agility, timing, planning avert brutality and force sport. Occasionally, suddenly, usually unaccountably, the primitive act of throwing or of striking results in terrible injury. The fear is never absent, the fear that randomness will take over. If hitting a major league fastball is the most difficult act in organized sport, the difficulty derives in part from the need to overcome fear in a split second.

The batter is, they say, on offense yet batting is essentially a reactive and deeply defensive act. The pitcher is, they say, on defense, yet the pitcher initiates play and controls the game ("Pitching is 75 percent of the game"). It is not clear, at least to me, finally who is on offense and who is on defense in baseball. The individual at the plate takes on, alone, the entire team on the field, including the catcher, who may actually control the game. The catcher is the only defensive player in any sport I know of whose defined position requires him to adopt the perspective, if not the stance, of the player on offense. Part of what a batter must overcome, part of the secretive, ruthless dimension of baseball, is the batter's knowledge that an opposing player, crouching right behind him, signals wordlessly in order to exploit his weaknesses. Is it so clear who is the defense, who is the offense? I think it is clear that part of the appeal of baseball is that at the outset it focuses on the individual with such clarity in such ambiguous circumstances.

If the game flows from the constantly reiterated, primitive confrontation of an individual with the world, represented by another solitary individual, nothing that ensues, except a home run—the dispositive triumph of one over the other, the surrogate kill—fails to involve the team. A strikeout involves the catcher and anything else brings the community, either on the bench or in the field, into play. And while the premium on individual effort is never lost, eventually the marvelous communal choreography of a team almost always takes over. As soon as a batter becomes a runner, he begins to compensate for the privileged perspective of the catcher by participating from his vantage point in the perspective of the other team. Every assigned role on the field potentially can, and often does, change with every pitch and with each kind of pitch or each ball hit fair. The subsequent complexities and potential interactions among all the players on the field expand in incalculable ways. When in the thrall of its communal aspects, hitting, stealing, and individual initiative give way to combined play-making, acts of sacrifice or cooperation, and obedience to signs and orders. Whether on offense or defense, the virtuoso is then subsumed into the company. The anarchic ways of solo operators are subdued by a free institution.

The ambiguities surrounding being on offense or defense, surrounding what it means to stand where you stand, endlessly re-create the American pageant of individual and group, citizen, and country. In baseball and daily life, Americans do not take sides so much as they change sides in ways checked and balanced. Finally, in baseball and daily life, regardless of which side you are on and where you stand, shared principles are supposed to govern.

Law, defined as a complex of formal rules, agreed-upon boundaries, authoritative arbiters, custom, and a system of symmetrical opportunities and demands, is enshrined in baseball. Indeed, the layout of the field shows baseball's essential passion for and reliance on precise proportions and clearly defined limits, all the better to give shape to energy and an arena for expression. The pitcher's rubber, 24 inches by 6 inches, is on a 15-inch mound in the middle of an 18-foot circle; the rubber is 60 feet 6 inches from home plate;

the four base paths are 90 feet long; the distance from first base to third, and home plate to second base, is 127 feet 3⅜ inches; the pitcher's rubber is the center of a circle, described by the arc of the grass behind the infield from foul line to foul line, whose radius is 95 feet; from home plate to backstop, and swinging in an arc, is 60 feet. On this square tipped like a diamond containing circles and contained in circles, built on multiples of 3, 9 players play 9 innings, with 3 outs to a side, each out possibly composed of 3 strikes. Four balls, four bases break (or is it underscore?), the game's reliance on "threes" to distribute an odd equality, all the numerology and symmetry tending to configure a game unbounded by that which bounds most sports, and adjudicates in many, time.

The game comes from an America where the availability of sun defined the time for work or play—nothing else. Virtually all our other sports reflect the time clock, either in their formal structure or their definition of a winner. Baseball views time as if it were an endlessly available resource; it may put a premium on speed, of throw or foot, but it is unhurried. Time, like the water and forests, like the land itself, is supposedly ever available.

The point is, symmetrical surfaces, deep arithmetical patterns, and a vast, stable body of rules designed to ensure competitive balance in the game, show forth a country devoted to equality of treatment and opportunity; a country whose deepest dream is of a divinely proportioned and peopled (the "threes" come from somewhere) green garden enclosure; above all, a country whose basic assertion is that law, in all its agreed-upon forms and manifestations, shall govern—not nature inexorable, for all she is respected, and not humankind's whims, for all that the game belongs to the people. Baseball's essential rules for place and for play were established, by my reckoning, with almost no exceptions of consequence, by 1895. By today, the diamond and the rules for play have the character of *données,* of Platonic ideas, of preexistent inevitabilities that encourage activity, contain energy, and, like any set of transcendent ideals, do not change.

Symbolic of this sensibility, the umpire in baseball has unique stature among sport's arbiters. Spectator and fan alike may, perhaps at times must, object to his judgment, his interpretation, his grasp of precedent, procedure, and relevant doctrine. Such dissent is encouraged, is valuable, and rarely, if ever, is successful. As instant replay shows, very rarely should it be. The umpire is untouchable (there is a law protecting his person) and infallible. He is the much maligned, indispensable, faceless figure of Judgment, in touch with all the codes, the lore, with nature's vagaries, for he decides when she has won. He is the Constitution and Court before your eyes, and he may be the most durable figure in the game for he, alone, never sits, never rests. He has no side, save the obligation to dispense justice speedily.

So much does our game tell us, about what we wanted to be, about what we are. Our character and our culture are reflected in this grand game. It would be foolish to think that all of our national experience is reflected in any single institution, even our loftiest, but it would not be wrong to claim for baseball a capacity to cherish individuality and inspire cohesion in a way that is a hallmark of our loftiest institutions. Nor would it be misguided to think that, however vestigial the remnants of our best hopes, we can still find, if we wish to, a moment called a game when those hopes have life, when each of us, those who are in and those out, has a chance to gather, in a green place around home.

IN 1987 KEVIN GROSS, *a pitcher for the Phillies, was ejected from a game and subsequently suspended for ten days for attaching a piece of sandpaper to his glove. The suspension was appealed. Roger Angell quotes Giamatti as commenting, "Last year I worked as hard on my response to the Kevin Gross Appeal as I worked on anything I did while I was in New Haven. It was challenging to try to be clear about cheating and what it meant, and to be fair at the same time." Giamatti's emphasis on the serious nature of premeditated guile presages that same concern two years later in the Pete Rose matter.*

DECISION IN
THE APPEAL OF
KEVIN GROSS

———————— ✦ ————————

*T*HE APPEAL OF MR. KEVIN GROSS OF THE
PHILADELPHIA PHILLIES OF HIS TEN-DAY
SUSPENSION FOR VIOLATING RULE 8.02 (B) IS
denied. He must begin serving his ten-day suspension
immediately.

The opinion that follows is more lengthy than is custom-
ary because the hearing giving rise to it was some five hours
long and involved exhibits of considerable breadth, two
entailing nearly 1,000 notations. Properly to deliberate upon
the materials and arguments requires extended examination,
as it required considerable time.

I. SUMMARY OF APPEAL

The Players Association (hereinafter P.A.) conceded that Mr. Gross had violated Official Playing Rule 8.02(b) by having sandpaper affixed to his glove and a sticky substance on his glove in the game of August 10, 1987. P.A. did not dispute that the president of the National League had the overall authority to interpret playing rules and impose discipline for infractions as provided in the Official Playing Rules (2.00 and 9.05[c]) and the National League Constitution (V.3.a and V.3.c). The burden of P.A.'s appeal was that the ten-day suspension was unduly harsh; it was, P.A. contended, without precedent, inconsistent with past practice, and not comparable with discipline for other offenses.

In order to provide the basis for these arguments, P.A. introduced exhibits, derived from P.A. records, listing infractions and discipline imposed from 1978 to 1987 in the American League and the National League, and, derived from National League records, a listing of ejections from games from 1977 to 1987 for reasons other than fighting, arguing, bench clearing, etc., and the discipline imposed.

II. THE RECORD

Before weighing the arguments derived from this historical record, it is necessary—as with any historical record—to assess the reliability of the record itself. The record presented by P.A. shows omissions, inconsistencies, and trivial errors. To wit:

P.A.'s exhibits omit any notation of the ten-day suspension and fine imposed on 8/24/82 on Mr. G. Perry, appealed to the American League president on 9/9/82; appeal denied; suspension served and fine paid, beginning 9/17/82. Mr. Perry was charged with violating rules 3.02 and 8.02.

P.A. exhibits omit any notation of the ten-day suspension imposed on 10/01/80 on Mr. R. Honeycutt for violating rule 3.02; P.A. notes only the fine for that offense imposed on Mr. Honeycutt on 9/30/80. The letter of L.S. McPhail, Jr., to R. Honeycutt of 10/1/80 clarifies the record.

P.A. exhibits occasionally include discipline imposed on coaches and managers but more often omit suspensions and fines since 1978 on such nonplaying personnel. Fuller data were available in the material requested by P.A. from the

National League. One would have assumed such data to be relevant when one is searching for patterns and standards of league-imposed discipline.

P.A. exhibits are also inconsistent as between themselves. The American League exhibit lists discipline imposed only through 6/25/87, omitting at least two months of this season, while the National League exhibit lists discipline up through the case under appeal, that of Mr. Gross.

These comments would not be germane had not the exhibits formed the basis for the P.A.'s appeal on the ground of undue severity and had not the exhibits themselves occupied such a significant portion of the hearing. No adverse inference is intended or drawn from these omissions or inconsistencies.

III. THE ARGUMENTS

A. That a ten-day suspension is without precedent for violating rule 8.02(b) is true. Any discipline for violating rule 8.02(b) would be without precedent because all the exhibits show that in the last ten years of major league baseball, there have been no recorded violations of rule 8.02(b). Severity of discipline, or mildness of discipline, cannot fruitfully be argued from a vacuum.

B. We must consider the argument of P.A. counsel that the ten-day suspension of Mr. Gross is harsh or unduly severe because it is not comparable to discipline historically imposed for other offenses. The record (excluding Mr. Gross) shows there to have been 39 disciplinary acts in major league base-ball since 1978 involving suspensions and fines—21 in the A.L., 18 in the N.L. Of the 21 cases in the American League, 17 saw discipline imposed for in some way physically abus-ing umpires (9 instances) or for fighting with players or fans (8 instances). All 18 instances of discipline in the National League were imposed for some form of physical abuse to umpires (11) or for fighting with players or fans (7). For these physical and abusive acts, discipline in each case in both leagues included monetary fines and suspensions. Suspen-sions in the American League ran from two to four days; in the National League, from two to fifteen days.

The 4 cases in the American League not falling into the category of physical and abusive acts included the aforementioned ten-day suspensions and fines imposed for violating rule 3.02 on R. Honeycutt and imposed for violating rule 3.02 and 8.02 on G. Perry.

The vast majority (35 of 39) of instances of discipline involving suspension and fines in the last ten years were for some sort of violent or impulsive act. This is not surprising in a physical game played intensely by highly skilled and competitive professional athletes. While such acts, whatever their nature, can never be condoned or tolerated, it must be recognized that they grow often out of impulse, and the aggressive, volatile nature of the game and of those who play it. It would be most surprising if the preponderance of serious infractions, and attendant discipline, were of a different kind.

C. There is, however, in the record another category of offenses and discipline that involve cheating. Such acts are the result not of impulse, borne of frustration or anger or zeal as violence is, but are rather acts of a cool, deliberate, premeditated kind. Unlike acts of impulse or violence, intended at the moment to vent frustration or abuse another, acts of cheating are intended to alter the very conditions of play to favor one person. They are secretive, covert acts that strike at and seek to undermine the basic foundation of any contest declaring the winner—that all participants play under identical rules and conditions. Acts of cheating destroy that necessary foundation and thus strike at the essence of a contest. They destroy faith in the games' integrity and fairness; if participants and spectators alike cannot assume integrity and fairness, and proceed from there, the contest cannot in its essence exist.

Acts of physical excess, reprehensible as they are, often represent extensions of the very forms of physical exertion that are the basis for playing the game; regulation and discipline seek to contain, not expunge, violent effort in sport. Cheating, on the other hand, has no organic basis in the game and no origins in the act of playing. Cheating is contrary to the whole purpose of playing to determine a winner fairly and cannot be simply contained; if the game is to flourish and engage public confidence, cheating must be clearly condemned with an eye to expunging it.

D. The ten-year history of discipline in the American

League shows acts of cheating dealt with more severely than various physical acts of impulse or abuse. The ten-year history of discipline in the National League offers no guidance whatever for cheating, save for a warning to D. Sutton in 1978; it shows that on two occasions longer suspensions were imposed than that given to Mr. Gross. The ten-year history of major league baseball shows that regardless of the kind of offense, all 39 suspensions were accompanied by monetary fines.

To summarize broad categories of comparison: across ten years of major league baseball, where discipline included a suspension, we find cases of cheating treated very seriously, usually more seriously than other offenses; and we find suspensions of greater duration than the suspension imposed on Mr. Gross.

E. Is Mr. Gross to be compared to all previous offenders receiving suspensions and fines? If so, the data do not support the charge of excessive severity, for some have been suspended longer and all have been fined.

What of comparable cases of cheating? Messrs. Honeycutt and Sutton were suspended for damaging a baseball or delivering damaged balls in violation of rule 3.02, wherein it is mandated that a pitcher "shall be suspended automatically for ten days," whereas Mr. Gross was suspended under rule 8.02(b) where no suspension is mandated. P.A. counsel argued that the rule makers must have considered a violation of rule 3.02 a more serious offense than a violation of rule 8.02(b) because the former mandates a suspension beyond ejection, while the latter mandates only ejection. Therefore, either by imposing a sentence not mandated, or by imposing a sentence under rule 8.02(b) by inappropriate analogy to rule 3.02, the National League has imposed an improper, and unduly severe, punishment on Mr. Gross.

The arguments are not persuasive. If only those penalties prescribed in the Official Playing Rules should be imposed, then all past discipline that has exceeded prescribed penalties was in error. But that is manifestly not the case.

In the particular instance of arguing by analogy from rule 3.02, in order to say that rule 8.02(b) must be read as limiting the league president only to the penalty prescribed, one must ignore the fact that 3.02 does not prescribe a monetary fine such as was imposed on Messrs. Honeycutt and Perry. The argument from analogy fails because the analogy contradicts precisely the point P.A. counsel seemed to wish to establish by analogy. If the prescriptions of rule 3.02 did not constrain the American League president, it is therefore specious to argue that the model of prescriptions in rule 3.02 constrains a league president under 8.02(b), particularly where there is no contrary past practice.

It is impossible to argue seriousness of offense, or severity of discipline, by analogy or by whether the Official Playing Rules prescribe a penalty or not. Infractions must be judged in the light of the applicable rule on a case by case basis. Past practice must be taken into account, if and when it exists. So also must current circumstances be carefully considered. A league president must neither be captivated by the past nor indifferent to it, any more than he may be capricious in imposing discipline, either on the side of severity or of laxity.

IV. CONCLUSION

What did Kevin Gross do? He deliberately and flagrantly violated rule 8.02(b) by affixing a round piece of apparently heavy-duty sandpaper to the lower thumb or heel area of his glove. He also had a sticky substance on the top of the glove's thumb. Sandpaper is not some foreign substance (like shampoo or chewing gum) that conceivably could have been inadvertently acquired by storing a glove in a clubhouse locker. Clearly the sandpaper was not acquired and affixed to the lower thumb by accident nor does sandpaper come in that shape, or adhere to the heel area of a baseball glove in nature. A premeditated effort is required to affix sandpaper to a glove. Because those bringing the appeal on behalf of Mr. Gross chose not to call him as a witness, though he was present, we cannot know if Mr. Gross had any explanation to counter the presumption that he deliberately brought onto the field an illegal glove for any reason than the one the rule is intended to forbid.

Among other substances, sandpaper is used to deface baseballs. That is why foreign substances are forbidden under rule 8.02(b). The intent of the rule is to prevent a pitcher from having on his person or in his possession any foreign substance that could mar or deface or be used to mar or deface a baseball in that game or in any game.

It is cheating per se to have such a glove with sandpaper and sticky substance on the field. On August 10, 1987, Mr. Gross cheated by bringing on the field an illegal glove. It is not necessary actively or even inadvertently (such as could have occurred, given the placement of the sandpaper in the glove) to have defaced a baseball. That contingency is covered elsewhere in the rules. Mr. Gross is neither charged with defacing a baseball nor with throwing a defaced baseball. To be guilty of cheating is enough to have flagrantly and willfully violated 8.02(b).

Cheating is a very serious offense and merits serious discipline. I have expressed myself above as to the reasons why cheating has always been considered destructive of the essence of a contest designed to declare a winner. Cheating corrodes the integrity of any game. It undermines the assumption necessary to any game declaring a winner, that the contestants are playing fairly, i.e., under identical rules and conditions. It destroys public and participant confidence, morale, and goodwill. Mr. Gross acted with indifference to these principles.

Amidst a season marred, in my view, by allegations of "scuffed" balls and "corked" bats, amidst all the warnings against cheating of various kinds, Mr. Gross exhibited a reckless disregard for the reputation and good name of his teammates, club, and league and for the integrity of the game. He acted wrongly, in a serious fashion, and his suspension is merited. The appeal is denied.

SEPTEMBER 1, 1987

A. BARTLETT GIAMATTI, PRESIDENT
The National League of Professional Baseball Clubs

NOW ON THE INSIDE *of the game as president of the National League, Giamatti translates his older concerns about decline and corrosion into the mundane details that make attendance at sporting events in general, but baseball in particular, less pleasant and more hazardous. In this 1987 article from the* Boston Globe, *he dwells upon not the rules of the game, but the principles of conduct that both fans and management must honor to retain the spectator at the green field Giamatti reveres.*

TO SPORTS AND FANS: CLEAN UP YOUR ACT

◆

S PORTS, PROFESSIONAL AND AMATEUR, HAVE
*A PROBLEM THAT TRANSCENDS IN ITS LONG-
TERM IMPLICATIONS THE ISSUES OF OUTSIZED*
salaries or scandals in recruiting or problematic labor relations. It is the slow but steady deterioration of the environment in which sports take place. When the ambiance for a
sporting event begins to sour, people stay away.

Part of the purpose of going to a high school, college, or
professional sports contest is to enjoy the gathering, to see
and hear the crowd become a community, to cheer, to inter-
vene vocally, to swap stories and pleasantries and opinions
with those around you. It is a gathering of the tribe at one of

its fundamental rituals and it is meant to provide pleasure as well as release from daily cares. It is meant to be strenuous and relaxing, a break from work, a time to pass on to the next generation lore and a way of looking at life and to teach a form of pleasure.

But if you cannot park and be sure you or your car will be safe; or if you are ignored by ushers or unable to find a decent or thug-free restroom; or if you cannot watch a contest free from the constant assault of obscene language or a mindlessly insistent scoreboard, seemingly run by people who dare not let the contest speak for itself; or if your child cannot watch without passively ingesting marijuana clouds; of if there are fights in the stands and on the field or arena of play that subtly and insidiously fuel and feed off each other—then you begin to wonder why you came. As time goes on, the stands increasingly become the private preserve of the roughneck who came in order to drink too much, and for whom the contest is simply an outlet for the aggressive, ultimately antisocial, impulses that physical sports are meant to redirect into acceptable patterns.

We live in a society that is aging and that therefore remembers and expects leisure in the form of sporting events of a different, less nasty kind. It is also a society increasingly comfortable with new video technology, comfortable culturally and economically. Within the decade we will be able to purchase video cassettes from vending machines; we will have on our roofs lean-tos the size of deck chairs capable of pulling in televised signals from all over the country (or the globe). In ten years, the vast majority of the population in America that wants to consume leisure passively, with its eyes and ears, will do so at home. Such people, my guess is about seven out of ten of us, will have video rooms, enhanced sound, remarkable reception facilities, libraries of tapes—in our homes. There will be very few incentives to go out to the ballpark or hockey rink or basketball arena or football stadium if home is as coherent and "receptive" as it will be and if the public arenas and parks are as deeply disagreeable for families, decent young people, groups of neighbors, the elderly as they will be if they continue on their present course.

This is not a problem simply for the professional or big-time college venues; it afflicts high schools as well. Nor is the problem sport specific, though some sports have marketed gratuitous violence more obviously than others. What is happening is a deterioration of forms of public pleasures (and the concomitant rise of privatized leisure). It is occurring because those responsible for the management of the whole sporting event have been either indifferent to the total ambiance or have often subtly undermined their own sport by encouraging the savagery implicit (and contained) in contact sports to become predominant.

At the heart of the matter, however, is not the violence that officials either cannot contain or are discouraged from containing on the field or floor. Such violence in a mysterious way feeds off the environment more than it fuels it, though finally the relation between fan and participant, and who incites whom, is resistant to simple analysis.

I believe that at the heart of the deteriorating environment is excessive drinking. It must be stopped. Those who wish to enter a contest already drunk must be turned away; those sneaking in liquor if it is expressly forbidden must be stopped;

those who come only to drink in the stands and disrupt must be controlled or ejected. Whoever manages the stadium or venue, whether academic institution or city or county or private company, must train parking-lot attendants, ushers, and security people; must establish clear rules for the sale of alcohol and train concessionaires; must make the alcohol management policy and its attendant procedures part of a larger set of policies about parking, security, hospitality for fans, cleanliness of facilities, scoreboard management.

If the ambiance for the sporting event is not considered crucial by management, there is no reason to believe that fans will leave home and come out; there is no reason to believe that families will subject themselves to goons and call it fun; there is no reason to believe that in ten years' time the vast majority of those who care about the sport will see it anywhere but on a screen — at which point the nature of the game's transmission will have reshaped the contest in ways no one, now, wishes to see. The responsibility lies squarely with the management of publicly played sports to remember that without fans who enjoy being there, live, the whole enterprise does not exist.

THIS ESSAY WAS *first presented as one of the Cook Lectures on American Institutions at the School of Law at the University of Michigan in 1989 and was posthumously published in a monograph titled* Take Time for Paradise. *After more than a decade, and now facing the gritty decisions that fall to the commissioner of organized baseball, Giamatti returns to some of his older themes. This piece is at once more formal in its focus on the structure of the game and informal in its conclusion, where Giamatti transports us to the center of the lobby of the Marriott Hotel in St. Louis during the 1987 National League playoffs.*

BASEBALL
AS NARRATIVE

◆

*S*OME CONTESTS DERIVE DIRECTLY FROM WORK — WHERE ELSE DO CAREB THROWING OR RODEO EVENTS COME FROM? — SOME FROM war, like archery or fencing or, perhaps, the javelin throw, some from primitive forms of combat, like boxing or wrestling. But regardless whence a contest or sport derives, its appeal will be on very personal, not deeply historical, grounds. We will watch or play games or sports that reflect how we think of ourselves or that promote how we wish to be perceived.

Our pleasure, however, whose origins are far more difficult to discover than are the historical roots of any sport or game, is radically tangled up with our childhood. Much of what we love later in a sport is what it recalls to us about ourselves at our earliest. And those memories, now smoothed and bending away from us in the interior of ourselves, are not simply of childhood or of a childhood game. They are memories of our best hopes. They are memories of a time when all that would be better was before us, as a hope, and the hope was fastened to a game. One hoped not so much to be the best who ever played as simply to stay in the game and ride it wherever it would go, culling its rhythms and realizing its promises. That is, I think, what it means to remember one's best hopes, and to remember them in a game, and revive them whenever one sees the game played, long after playing is over.

I was led to these thoughts by thinking on my own love of baseball, and the origins of that emotion. And then I was led to this last chapter by the opening lines of a poem by Marianne Moore called "Baseball and Writing":

> *Fanaticism? No. Writing is exciting*
> *and baseball is like writing.*
> *You can never tell with either*
> *how it will go*
> *or what you will do.*

Serendipity is the essence of both games, the writing one and baseball. But is not baseball more than *like* writing? Is not baseball a form of writing? Is that not why so many writers love baseball? To answer this question, we will turn third and test our initial assumptions.

If it is instructive as well as pleasurable to think about how America produces and consumes its leisure, then I believe thinking about baseball will tell us about ourselves as a people. Such thoughts will test two propositions. The first is that baseball, in all its dimensions, best mirrors the *condition of freedom* for Americans that Americans ever guard and aspire to. The second proposition is that because baseball simulates and stimulates the condition of freedom, Americans identify the game with the country. Even those indifferent to baseball, or country, or those who scorn them, at some level know them. The rest of us love them.

To know baseball is to continue to aspire to the condition of freedom, individually, and as a people, for baseball is grounded in America in a way unique to our games. Baseball is part of America's plot, part of America's mysterious, underlying design—the plot in which we all conspire and collude, the plot of the story of our national life. Our national plot is to be free enough to consent to an order that will enhance and compound—as it constrains—our freedom. That is our grounding, our national story, the tale America tells the world. Indeed, it is the story we tell ourselves. I believe the story in its outline and many of its episodes. By repeating again the outline of the American Story, and placing baseball within it, we engage the principle of narrative. We posit an old story, sufficiently ordered by the imagination so that the principle of design or purpose may emerge.

What are the narrative principles of baseball, its over-plot? At its most abstract, baseball believes in ordering its energies, its contents, around threes and fours. It believes that symmetry surrounds meaning, but even more, forces meaning. Symmetry, a version of equality, forces and sharpens competition. Symmetrical demands in a symmetrical setting encourage both passion and precision.

We see this quality best when we consider baseball's plot not as story line, but plot as soil, the concrete grounding.

The field, the literal plot of the game, consists of a square whose four sides are ninety feet long; this square is tipped so that a "diamond" is encased in the grass. Not quite in the middle of the square, sixty feet, six inches from home plate, is a circle, with a radius of nine feet, at whose center (we are on the pitcher's mound) is a "rectangular slab of whitened rubber, 24 inches by six inches." (The distance from the pitcher's rubber to the front edge of home plate is fifty-nine feet, one inch. The rubber itself is one inch behind the center of the pitcher's mound.) So far, all the dimensions are multiples of three.

This last rectangle is the central shape in the geometry of the field, set within but not parallel to the larger square of the "diamond." The circle of the mound faces a larger circle around home plate, whose radius is thirteen feet, containing three squares, two of which, for batters, are six feet by four feet. The third is marked only on three sides, is forty-three inches wide, and is of undetermined length.

The square of the diamond is contained in a larger arc or partial circle, whose radius, measured from the center of the rectangular pitcher's slab, is ninety-five feet. The perimeter of this (partial) circle denotes the grass line running from foul line to foul line at the outer infield or innermost outfield. The bases are rectangular, fifteen inches square. The foul lines extend from the tip of home plate along the sides of the ninety-foot square to first and third. These perpendicular lines theoretically extend to infinity. In fact, since June 1, 1958, they are obliged to extend at least 325 feet until their path is interrupted by a fence (just as there must be a minimum of four hundred feet in the line from home plate to the center-field fence).

How to characterize the structural principles grounding this game? Squares containing circles containing rectangles; precision in counterpoint with passion; order compressing energy. The potentially universal square, whose two sides are foul (actually fair) lines, partially contains the circle, whose radius is at least four hundred feet and whose perimeter is the circle of the fence from foul line to foul line, which contains the circle of the outer infield grass, which contains the square of the diamond, containing the circle of the pitcher's mound and squares of the three bases. The circle of the mound contains the rectangle of the pitcher's slab and faces the circle of the home-plate area, which contains the rectangles of the batter's boxes and the area for umpire and catcher. At the center of this circle, and existing in eternal tension with the pitcher's rectangle—seemingly the center of such power, of so many dimensions—is the source of the macro dimensions, the point of reference for all the medium and the larger geometric shapes, the only shape on the field that does not figure the eternal and universal outlines and meanings of square and circle. We are at home plate, the center of all the universes, the *omphalos,* the navel of the world. It, too, plays around fours and threes, but altered, a shape unique. The *Official Baseball Rules:*

Home base shall be marked by a five-sided slab of whitened rubber. It shall be a 17-inch square with two of the corners removed so that one edge is 17 inches long, two adjacent sides are 8½ inches and the remaining two sides are 12 inches and set at an angle to make a point. It shall be set in the ground with the point at the intersection of the lines extending from home base to first base and to third base; with the 17-inch edge facing the pitcher's plate, and the two 12-inch edges coinciding with the first and third base lines. (1.05)

This curious pentagram is central in every sense to the concentric circles and contending rectangles of the place. It is also deeply disruptive of their classic proportions and their exquisitely choreographed positions and appositions. Home plate mysteriously organizes the field as it energizes the odd patterns of squares tipped and circles incomplete. Home plate radiates a force no other spot on the field possesses, for its irregular precision, its character as an incomplete square but finished pentagram, starts the field, if you will, playing. It begins the dance of line and circle, the encounters of energy direct and oblique, of misdirection and confrontation, of boundary and freedom that is the game, before any player sets foot on the field. Home plate also has a peculiar significance for it is the goal of both teams, the single place that in territorially based games—games about conquering—must be symbolized by two goals or goal lines or nets or baskets. In baseball, everyone wants to arrive at the same place, which is where they start.

In baseball, even opponents gather at the same curious, unique place called home plate. Catcher and batter, siblings who may see the world separately but share the same sight lines, are backed up and yet ruled by the parent figure, the umpire, whose place is the only one not completely defined. This tense family clusters at home, facing the world together, each with separate responsibilities and tasks and perspectives, each with different obligations and instruments. Some are intent on flight, some on communication, some simply on the good order of it all — the "conduct of the game" — but they are still a family or family-like group in their proximity, their overall perspective, their chatter and squabbling, their common desire, differently expressed, to master the ferocity and duplicity of that spherical, irrational reality — the major league pitch.

But I anticipate. The geometry of the field that extends the threes and fours gives as well the deep patterns that order the narrative — three strikes, three bases, nine players, nine innings; four bases (including home) or four balls (the walk which is escape, the commencement of movement that might fulfill the quaternity of the diamond). Three and its multiples work in baseball to delimit, to constrain, to be the norm that, except for duration, cannot be surpassed. Only nine innings may be lawfully overgone—baseball having no clock and, indeed moving counterclockwise, so anxious is it to establish its own rhythms and patterns independent of clock time. (Although see *Official Baseball Rules,* 8.03 and 8.04, setting time limits of pitchers.) But even that extension beyond nine exists because there must be a winner, an ending, that is definitive. How a game ends is itself interesting; the closure of any narrative always is. Baseball ends with the home team having the final say, the guests having opened the narrative.

The central triad of strikes and outs telescopes out into three by three, giving us a game with a definite beginning, middle, and end, a well-made play in three acts, of six scenes to an act, three to a side. Put another way, if three strikes were the lot of every batter on one side, then twenty-seven batters would have to go up and down on one side to fulfill a perfect game. But there is a greater perfection—that the maximum of twenty-seven, which is also a minimum, go up and go down for both sides. That ultimately perfect game could theoretically endure in time like the foul lines in space—indefinitely. Our mediation has found the One, but where is the game?

If extrapolation may drive baseball's organizing numerology and patterns to a sterile (and impossible) perfection, only repetition can bring satisfaction. The game on the field is repetitious—pitch after pitch, swing after swing, player after player, out succeeding out, half inning making whole inning, top to bottom to top, the patterns accumulating and making organizing principles, all around and across those precise shapes in and on the earth. Organized by the metric of the game, by the prosody of the play, is all the random, unpredictable, explosive energy of playing, crisscrossing the precise shapes in lines and curves, bounces and wild hops and parabolas and slashing arcs. There is a ferocity to a slide, a whispering, exploding sound to a fastball, a knife-edged danger to a ball smashed at a pitcher—there is a violence in the game at variance with its formal patterns, a hunger for speed at variance with its leisurely pace, a potential for irrational randomness at variance with its geometric shapes.

The game is all counterpoint. The precise lines and bound-aries and rules, and all the scholastic precision baseball brings to bear on any question, on every play, only serve to constrain the sudden eruptions of energy, the strenuosity of the game, and thus to compound the meaning and joy of accomplishment. We recall that the patterns of rhyme and the rules for pivot and recapitulation in a sonnet compress the energy of language, and compound significance. But cannot the same be said of turning a double play, where the rhythm and force, pivot and repetition are the whole point? The point being that freedom is the fulfillment of the promise of an energetic, complex order?

If baseball is a Narrative, it is like others—a work of imag-ination whose deeper structures and patterns of repetition force a tale, oft-told, to fresh and hitherto-unforeseen mean-ing. But what is the nature of the tale oft-told that recom-mences with every pitch, with every game, with every season? That patiently accrues its tension and new meaning with every iteration? It is the story we have hinted at already, the story of going home after having left home, the story of how difficult it is to find the origins one so deeply needs to find. It is the literary mode called Romance.

While it may be fanciful to construe the cluster around the plate as a family, it is certainly not a fancy to call that place "home." That is the name of the odd-shaped pentagram. Home plate or home base. I do not know where it clearly acquired that name. I know that the earliest accounts of the game, or an early version of it, in children's books of games in the early nineteenth century, call the points around the field — often marked by posts — "bases." The game was called "base," though in his diary a soldier at Valley Forge with Washington called it "baste." I know Jane Austen tells us at the beginning of *Northanger Abbey* that Catherine Morland played "base ball" as well as cricket, thus distinguishing them. But none of these early references clarifies whence came the name for "home." Why is home plate not called fourth base? As far as I can tell, it has ever been thus.

And why not? Meditate upon the name. *Home* is an English word virtually impossible to translate into other tongues. No translation catches the associations, the mixture of memory and longing, the sense of security and autonomy and accessibility, the aroma of inclusiveness, of freedom from wariness, that cling to the word *home* and are absent from *house* or even *my house. Home* is a concept, not a place; it is a state of mind where self-definition starts; it is origins — the mix of time and place and smell and weather wherein one first realizes one is an original, perhaps *like* others, especially those one loves, but discrete, distinct, not to be copied. Home is where one first learned to be separate and it remains in the mind as the place where reunion, if it ever were to occur, would happen.

So home drew Odysseus, who then set off again because it is not necessary to be in a specific place, in a house or town, to be one who has gone home. So home is the goal — rarely glimpsed, almost never attained — of all the heroes descended from Odysseus. All literary romance derives from the *Odyssey* and is about rejoining — rejoining a beloved, rejoining parent to child, rejoining a land to its rightful owner or rule. Romance is about putting things aright after some tragedy has put them asunder. It is about restoration of the right relations among things—and going home is where that restoration occurs because that is where it matters most.

In America, the cluster of associations around the word, and its compounds, is perhaps more poignant because of the extraordinary mobility of the American people. From the beginning, we have been a nation constantly moving. As I have suggested elsewhere, the concept of home has a particular resonance for a nation of immigrants, all of whom left one home to seek another; the idea of a "homestead" established a frontier, the new home beyond the home one left in the East; everyone has a "hometown" back there, at least back in time, where stability or at least its image remains alive.

Stability, origins, a sense of oneness, the first clearing in the woods—to go home may be impossible but it is often a driving necessity, or at least a compelling dream. As the heroes of romance beginning with Odysseus know, the route is full of turnings, wanderings, danger. To attempt to go home is to go the long way around, to stray and separate in the hope of finding completeness in reunion, freedom in reintegration with those left behind. In baseball, the journey begins at home, negotiates the twists and turns at first, and often flounders far out at the edges of the ordered world at rocky second—the farthest point from home. Whoever remains out there is said to "die" on base. Home is finally beyond reach in a hostile world full of quirks and tricks and hostile folk. There are no dragons in baseball, only shortstops, but they can emerge from nowhere to cut one down.

And when it is given one to round third, a long journey seemingly over, the end in sight, then the hunger for home, the drive to rejoin one's earlier self and one's fellows, is a pressing, growing, screaming in the blood. Often the effort fails, the hunger is unsatisfied as the catcher bars fulfillment, as the umpire-father is too strong in his denial, as the impossibility of going home again is reenacted in what is often baseball's most violent physical confrontation, swift, savage, down in the dirt, nothing availing.

Or if the attempt, long in planning and execution, works, then the reunion and all it means is total—the runner is a returned hero, and the teammates are for an instant all true family. Until the attempt is tried again. A "home run" is the definitive kill, the overcoming of obstacle at one stroke, the gratification instantaneous in knowing one has earned a risk-free journey out, around, and back—a journey to be taken at a leisurely pace (but not too leisurely) so as to savor the freedom, the magical invulnerability, from denial or delay.

Virtually innumerable are the dangers, the faces of failure one can meet if one is fortunate enough even to leave home. Most efforts fail. Failure to achieve the first leg of the voyage is extremely likely. In no game of ours is failure so omnipresent as it is for the batter who would be the runner. The young batter who would light out from home, so as to return bearing fame and the spoils of success, is most often simply out, unable to leave and therefore never to know until the next try whether he or she can ever be more than simply a vessel of desire.

The tale of leaving and seeking home is told in as many ways as one can imagine, and there still occur every season plays on the field that even the most experienced baseball people say they have never seen before. The random events, the variety of incidents, the different ways various personalities react to pressure, the passion poured into the quest to win—all are organized by the rhythms of the innings, by the metric of the count and the pitcher's rhythm, and by the cool geometry that is underfoot and overarching.

Repetition within immutable lines and rules; baseball is counterpoint: stability vying with volatility, tradition with the quest for a new edge, ancient rhythms and ever-new blood—an oft-told tale, repeated in every game in every season, season after season. If this is the tale told, who tells it? Clearly, the players who enact it thereby also tell it. But the other true tellers of the narrative are those for whom it is played. If baseball is a narrative, an epic of exile and return, a vast, communal poem about separation, loss, and the hope for reunion—if baseball is a Romance Epic—it is finally told by the audience. It is the Romance Epic of homecoming America sings to itself.

Where does America sing this poem, say this story? Wherever baseball gathers. Let me tell you of one gathering that will stand for all the others, for while we have considered the abstract principles and patterns of our narrative, and its mythic fable, it is meet to be most concrete when thinking on the tellers of the tale, for in them, too, the narrative lives.

The Marriott Pavilion Hotel in St. Louis is hard by the ballpark. It consists of a pair of towers linked by a vast lobby and corridors and a ramp, the cavernous space interspersed with plants and some chairs and columns, the floor of this cavern covered by a carpeting the color of a fresh bruise. During the National League Championship Series between St. Louis and San Francisco in 1987, the lobby was ablaze — with Cardinal crimson on hats, jackets, sweaters, scarves, ties. Here and there one glimpsed the orange-and-black of the House of Lurie, as a Giant rooter, like some lonely fish, wove its way across a scarlet coral reef, alive and breathing in the cavernous deep. But such creatures were rare.

By mid-morning, the lobby is crowded, and will remain crowded, except during the game, until about 2 A.M., then to fill up by nine and wait the long day until game time. There are the smiling, middle-aged couples, festooned in buttons and insignia, this day yet another convention day in a life-time of conventioneering; the groups of teenage boys, in the plumage of scarlet windbreakers, like young birds craning their necks for the nourishment of a glimpse; a trio of natty young men, one with a briefcase, who are—I learn later from a hapless friend—pickpockets. They work the elevators, one to hold the door, one to feign having caught his shoe in the crack between floor and car, one to lift the wallet of the first person to assist. By a plant or a coffee shop, always alone, white hair crisply permed, in electric blue or purple pants suit, holding an autograph book, is a grandmotherly woman, smiling distractedly, waiting for a hero. There are always some single men in their forties, in nondescript clothes, hair slightly awry, eyes burning with fatigue and anticipation; they are the religiously obsessed, drawn by a vision in their heads that will not give them peace. They stand apart and wait for hours in this holy place. Very different are the middle-aged teen-agers, men in groups, all mid-forties, who shout and drink the day away, some with young women in black leather pants and scarlet T-shirts, their laughter and their manner frenzied. At the back of the lobby, down on a lower level, around a low table, sit this morning the Giant's manager and coaches.

They are like chiefs at a gathering of the clan, planning strategy, ignoring the celebrants while absorbing their energy.

Across the lobby of the Marriott Pavilion Hotel march in precision a group of young people, all in their twenties, network technicians off to work. The men are all bearded, in down jackets and jeans, the women in sweaters and beads and leg warmers. All wear some kind of boot. They are the flower children of High Tech. The future is theirs and they know it. They stride, silent and confident, like trainees at McKinsey. The chosen.

The largest contingent, in groups of three or four, is men in middle age and older, in suits and resplendent ties and polished shoes, some with cigars; they have seamed faces and eyes that seem to squint even in shade. They stand with the poised patience born of watching a dozen thousand baseball games — the scouts, the farm directors, the active or former coaches, the minor league general managers, retired ballplayers or umpires, former managers, the sporting goods representatives who once played the outfield. These are the true Baseball people. Among them one spots a younger face, the front office worker with a club, someone in PR or Promotion, some assistant to a general manager. There is an owner here and there, a broadcaster in his plumage, a club financial officer, a Director of Player Development representing his team at the Series. There are corporate sponsors, an occasional agent, someone's glistening lawyer, a television executive. And through it all, recognizable by their rumpled casualness and weary eyes, are the working press, mostly the beat writers and columnists, occasionally a magazine writer—the daily press in mismatched jackets and trousers, shirts open, barely recovered from filing, always looking for the next hook, the next lead, the telling anecdote. Distracted, intense, listening to three conversations and holding forth in two, the journalists circulate according to a pecking order known only to them. When they sit, it is as if there were a cosmic seating chart; no one is ever in the wrong group. Now they move through the crowd as the crowd shifts and eddies and pauses and waits, anticipating the next game, replaying last night's contest, last week's, last year's.

Add the groupies, the sharpies, the hangers-on, the family

members, the deal-makers, the ticket hustlers, the fathers who aim and loose their children like heat-seeking missiles to bring down an autograph, the busloads of one-time fans, bewildered and giddy—in short, everyone but the players, who never appear in the lobby until it is all over—and the sound is a high, constant hum, a vast buzz of a million bees, the sound almost palpable and, for hours, never varying in pitch or intensity as anecdote vies with anecdote or joke or gossip or monologue or rude ribbing, so reminiscent of the clubhouse. It is the sound of tip and critique and prediction and second-guessing, of nasty crack and generous assessment, of memory cutting across memory, supplementing and correcting and coloring the tale, all the crosscutting, overlapping, salty, blunt, nostalgic, sweet conversation about only one subject—Baseball.

Here the oft-told tale that is the game is told again. It is told always in the present tense, in a paratactic style that reflects the game's seamless, cumulative character, each event linked to the last and creating the context for the next—a style almost Biblical in its continuity and instinct for typology. It is told in a tone at once elegiac, sharply etched, inclusive of all nuance. Baseball people have the keenest eyes for the telling detail I have ever known. This might be an overheard moment—one erect, white-haired old man to two peers:

"So now Tebbetts is catching in Boston, he tells me last winter, and Parnell is pitching, it's against New York, and it's a brutal day, no wind, hot, rainy, it's going to pour and they want to get the game in, and Joe Gordon splits his thumb going into second when Junior Stevens steps on his hand, he can't pivot, and now it's the eighth, tie score, and Bobby Brown comes up with two out and Bauer sitting on third and Birdie says to Ed Hurley who's got the plate, 'This is the Doctor, Ed, this is a left-handed doctor . . .'" And it goes on, extending itself by loops and symmetrical segments and reiterations just the way the game does, as if it were yesterday and not August 1949.

Such is the talk in the lobby of the Marriott Pavilion Hotel in St. Louis during the League Championship Series in the first week of October 1987, as it was also in lobbies in San Francisco and Detroit and Minneapolis, as it is every time

Baseball gathers—whether in clubhouse, bus, or airplane. This is the talk in lobbies across some two thousand games a season, as it has been season after season, since the 1870s, before artificial turf and domes, before air travel, before night baseball—back to the days of trains and rooming houses and front porches, the first versions of the lobby.

So Ned Hanlon must have talked, and McGraw, and Speaker and Miller Huggins and even Connie Mack; so Sisler may have talked and Jackie, surely Durocher and Stengel, and so talk Yogi and Ernie and Whitey and Lasorda and Cashen and Sparky and Willie Mays and all the thousands they entail; the players and coaches and scouts and managers and umpires, somewhere they all talk. But the fullest, most expansive, most public talk is the talk in the lobby, baseball's second-favorite venue. The lobby is the park of talk; it is the enclosed place where the game is truly told, because told again and again. Each time it is played and replayed in the telling, the fable is refined, the nuances burnished the color of old silver. The memories in baseball become sharpest as they recede, for the art of telling improves with age.

Let me close in the tone and style of our national narrative: So now, I'm standing in the lobby of the Marriott in St. Louis in October of '87 and I see this crowd, so happy with itself, all talking baseball, and I want to be in this game, so I spend two hours moving about, listening to them talk the game and hearing them getting it right, working at the fine points the way players in the big leagues do, and it comes to me slowly, around noon, that this, *this,* is what Aristotle must have meant by the imitation of an action.

✦ ✦ ✦

The following was written as an epilogue to *Take Time for Paradise.*

Beginning with the conviction that our use of "free time" told us about ourselves as a people, I posed — more for myself thinking on baseball than to persuade the reader — the question: Is not freedom the fulfillment of the promise of an energetic, complex order? Clearly I believe the answer is yes, and clearly, therefore, I believe we cherish as Americans a game wherein freedom and reunion are both possible. Baseball fulfills the promise America made itself to cherish the individual while recognizing the overarching claims of the group. It sends its players out in order to return again, allowing all the freedom to accomplish great things in a dangerous world. So baseball restates a version of America's promises every time it is played. The playing of the game is a restatement of the promises that we can all be free, that we can all succeed.

So games, contests, sports reiterate the purpose of freedom every time they are enacted—the purpose being to show how to be free and to be complete and connected, unimpeded and integrated, all at once. That is the role of leisure, and if leisure were a god, rather than Aristotle's version of the highest human state, sport would be a constant reminder—not a faded remnant—of the transcendent or sacred being. This is so because sport—no matter how cheapened (and it need not be) or commercialized (and it often is) or distant from an external ideal (which it may never have approached)—contains within itself, as a self-transforming activity, fueled by instinct and intellect alike, the motive for freedom. The very elaborations of a sport—its internal conventions of all kinds, its ceremonies, its endless meshes entangling itself—are for the purpose of training and testing (perhaps by defeating) and rewarding the rousing motion within us to find a moment (or more) of freedom. Freedom is that state where energy and order merge and all complexity is purified into a simple coherence, a fitness of parts and purpose and passions that cannot be surpassed and whose goal could only be to be itself.

If we have known freedom, then we love it; if we love freedom, then we fear, at some level (individually or collectively), its loss. And then we cherish sport. As our forebears did, we remind ourselves through sport of what, here on earth, is our noblest hope. Through sport, we re-create our daily portion of freedom, in public.

PETE ROSE, ONE *of the great players in twentieth-century baseball, was an infielder for the Cincinnati Reds before becoming manager in 1989. Allegations of gambling, and especially betting on baseball — and on his own team — were leveled at Rose that same year. Bitter legal conflicts ensued on both sides, and Giamatti was accused of bias against Rose. The public, too, was polarized. Though Pete Rose never admitted guilt, ultimately, he and Giamatti reached an agreement that banned Rose from baseball for life. Giamatti agonized over the charges. Though Giamatti's words are spare, his sincerity and seriousness are evident in this statement on one of baseball's darkest chapters since the Black Sox scandal in 1919. This final written utterance was issued one week before his death in 1989.*

STATEMENT RELEASED TO THE PRESS ON THE PETE ROSE MATTER

◆

*T*HE BANISHMENT FOR LIFE OF PETE ROSE FROM BASEBALL IS THE SAD END OF A SORRY EPISODE. ONE OF THE GAME'S GREATEST players has engaged in a variety of acts which have stained the game, and he must now live with the consequences of those acts. By choosing not to come to a hearing before me, and by choosing not to proffer any testimony or evidence contrary to the evidence and information contained in the report of the special counsel to the commissioner, Mr. Rose has accepted baseball's ultimate sanction, lifetime ineligibility.

This sorry episode began last February when baseball

received firm allegations that Mr. Rose bet on baseball games and on the Reds' games. Such grave charges could not and must never be ignored. Accordingly, I engaged, and Mr. Ueberroth appointed, John Dowd as special counsel to investigate these and any other allegations that might arise and to pursue the truth wherever it took him. I believed then and believe now that such a process, whereby an experienced professional inquires on behalf of the commissioner as the commissioner's agent, is fair and appropriate. To pretend that serious charges of any kind can be responsibly examined by a commissioner alone fails to recognize the necessity to bring professionalism and fairness to any examination and the complexity a private entity encounters when, without judicial or legal powers, it pursues allegations in the complex real world.

Baseball had never before undertaken such a process because there had not been such grave allegations since the time of Landis. If one is responsible for protecting the integrity of the game of baseball—that is, the game's authenticity, honesty, and coherence—then the process one uses to protect the integrity of baseball must itself embody that integrity. I sought by means of a special counsel of proven professionalism and integrity, who was obliged to keep the subject of the investigation and his representatives informed about key information, to create a mechanism whereby the integrity we sought to protect was itself never violated. Similarly, in writing to Mr. Rose on May 11, I designed, as is my responsibility, a set of procedures for a hearing that would have afforded him every opportunity to present statements or testimony of witnesses or any other evidence he saw fit to answer the information and evidence presented in the Report of the Special Counsel and its accompanying materials.

That Mr. Rose and his counsel chose to pursue a course in the courts rather than appear at hearings scheduled for May 25 and then June 26, and then chose to come forward with a stated desire to settle this matter is now well known to all. My purpose in recounting the process and the procedures animating that process is to make two points that the American public deserves to know:

First, that the integrity of the game cannot be defended

except by a process that itself embodies integrity and fairness;

Second, should any other occasion arise where charges are made or acts are said to be committed that are contrary to the interests of the game or that undermine the integrity of baseball, I fully intend to use such a process and procedure to get to the truth and, if need be, to root out offending behavior. I intend to use, in short, every lawful and ethical means to defend and protect the game.

I say this so that there may be no doubt about where I stand or why I stand there. I believe baseball is a beautiful and exciting game, loved by millions — I among them — and I believe baseball is an important, enduring American institution. It must assert and aspire to the highest principles — of integrity, of professionalism of performance, of fair play within its rules. It will come as no surprise that like any institution composed of human beings, this institution will not always fulfill its highest aspirations. I know of no earthly institution that does. But this one, because it is so much a part of our history as a people and because it has such a purchase on our national soul, has an obligation to the people for whom it is played — to its fans and well-wishers — to strive for excellence in all things and to promote the highest ideals.

I will be told that I am an idealist. I hope so. I will continue to locate ideals I hold for myself and for my country in the national game as well as in other of our national institutions. And while there will be debate and dissent about this or that or another occurrence on or off the field, and while the game's nobler parts will always be enmeshed in the human frailties of those who, whatever their role, have stewardship of this game, let there be no doubt or dissent about our goals for baseball or our dedication to it. Nor about our vigilance and vigor — and patience — in protecting the game from blemish or stain or disgrace.

The matter of Mr. Rose is now closed. It will be debated and discussed. Let no one think that it did not hurt baseball. That hurt will pass, however, as the great glory of the game asserts itself and a resilient institution goes forward. Let it also be clear that no individual is superior to the game.